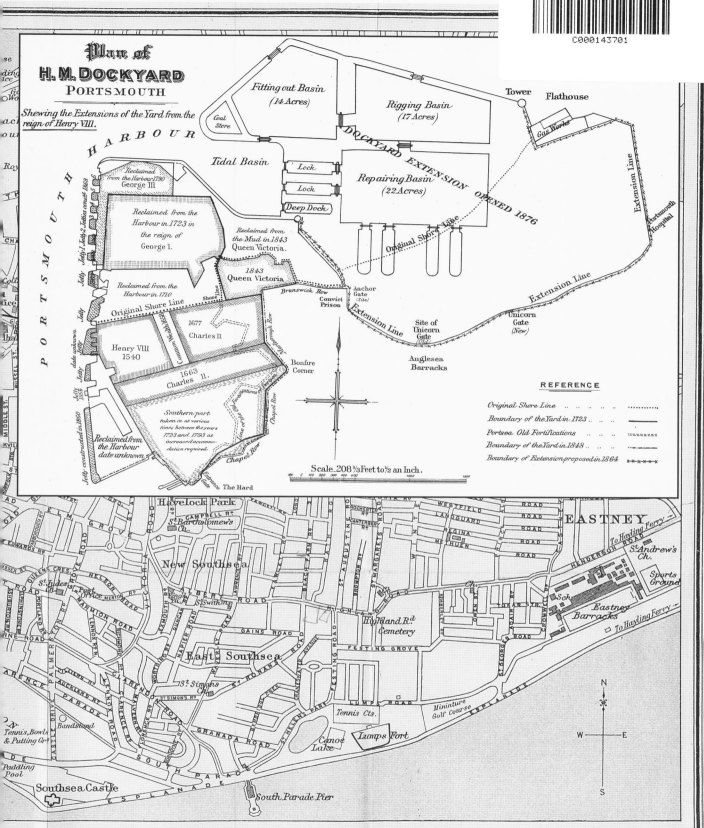

Plan of
H.M. DOCKYARD
PORTSMOUTH

Shewing the Extensions of the Yard from the reign of Henry VIII.

Fitting out Basin
(14 Acres)

Rigging Basin
(17 Acres)

Tower   Flathouse

Coal Store

Gas Works

Tidal Basin

Lock

Lock

DOCKYARD EXTENSION OPENED 1876

Repairing Basin
(22 Acres)

Extension Line

Deep Dock

PORTSMOUTH HARBOUR

Reclaimed from the Harbour 1790
George III

Reclaimed from the Harbour in 1723 in the reign of George I.

Reclaimed from the Mud in 1843
Queen Victoria.

Original Shore Line

Portsmouth Hospital

Reclaimed from the Harbour in 1710

1843
Queen Victoria

Brunswick Row
Convict Prison

Anchor Gate (Site)

Extension Line

Original Shore Line

Jetty 1 Jetty 2 Jetties constd. 1868

Jetty

Jetty date unknown

Jetty

Shore

Marlborough Row

1677
Charles II

Site of Unicorn Gate (Old)

Unicorn Gate
(New)

Henry VIII
1540

Common Hard constructed 1856

1663
Charles II.

Bonfire Corner

Anglesea Barracks

Jetty 1856

Jetty constructed in 1860

Southern part taken in at various times between the years 1723 and 1793 as increased accommodation required.

Line of the Old Fortifications of Portsea

Chapel Row

Reclaimed from the Harbour date unknown

Jetty constructed date unknown

Chapel Row

Entrance Gate

The Hard

Scale, 208⅓ Feet to ½ an Inch.

REFERENCE

Original Shore Line	. . . . .
Boundary of the Yard in 1723	. . . .
Portsea Old Fortifications	. . . . .
Boundary of the Yard in 1848	. . . .
Boundary of Extension proposed in 1864	x x x x x

Havelock Park

St Bartholomew's Ch.

WESTFIELD ROAD

LANDGUARD ROAD

EASTNEY

New Southsea

CANTERBURY

REGINA

METHUEN

To Hayling Ferry

St Andrew's Ch.

Sports Ground

St Jude's

Post Office

St Swithin

Highland Rd. Cemetery

Eastney Barracks

East Southsea

St Simons Ch.

FESTING GROVE

To Hayling Ferry

St Simon's Rd.

GAINS ROAD

HIGHLAND ROAD

GRANADA ROAD

LUMPS ROAD

Miniature Golf Course

N

Tennis, Bowls & Putting Gr.

Bandstand

Tennis Cts.

Lumps Fort

W   E

Paddling Pool

SOUTH PARADE

ESPLANADE

Canoe Lake

S

Southsea Castle

ESPLANADE

South Parade Pier

PORTSMOUTH

In Defence of the Realm

Po

RTSMOUTH

In Defence of the Realm

John Sadden

with best wishes

John Sadden

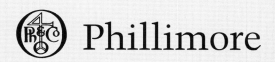 Phillimore

2001

Published by
PHILLIMORE & CO. LTD.
Shopwyke Manor Barn, Chichester, West Sussex

ISBN 1 86077 165 3

Previous page: Aerial view of Point, 1979, showing something of the historical impact of defence on Portsmouth's topography. In the foreground is HMS *Vernon*'s heliport, Vulcan Building (formerly the Gunwharf's Grand Storehouse) and diving tower, Vosper Thorneycroft, shipbuilding in the Inner Camber, and coastal fortifications including the Round and Square Towers. Grand Parade, the Royal Garrison Church and Governor's Green are visible in the distance

Printed and bound in Great Britain by
BUTLER AND TANNER LTD
London and Frome

CONTENTS

For Karen

ACKNOWLEDGEMENTS

I would like to thank a number of individuals who have assisted in the preparation of this book, including Keith Hartley of DERA (Haslar), Julie Denyer, librarian of the Hampshire Navy Collection (Gosport), Allison Wareham, librarian of the Royal Naval Museum Library (Portsmouth) and Stephen Grace, librarian of Southampton Local Studies Collection. I am also indebted to David Francis and Janet Cox for their helpful comments. Thanks are also due to the staffs of Portsmouth Naval and Local Studies Collection, Hampshire Local Studies Collection (Winchester), Hampshire County Libraries (Gosport, Fareham and Petersfield Libraries), Portsmouth Record Office, Hampshire Record Office, HMS *Collingwood*, HMS *Sultan*, the D-Day Museum and the Imperial War Museum, the British Library, the University of Portsmouth and Portsmouth City Engineer's Department. Acknowledgement is also made to the research of William Gates, on which I have relied heavily, and the many illustrators and photographers whose work is included, most notably the postcard photographers Stephen Cribb, J.C. Lawrence, Welch, Humphries, Cozons, Blake Frank Powell, Edgar Ward and William Burbage.

Picture Credits

Chapter 1

FORTIFICATIONS

1
Portchester Castle.

The fear of invasion and the desire to safeguard ships in harbour have been constant motivating forces for the establishment and maintenance of fortifications in the Portsmouth area since the building of Portchester Castle in the third century. Between wars, the fabric of defence was often neglected as peacetime priorities took over and the relentless slide into obsolescence of arms and fortifications went unchecked. But when the next potential crisis emerged the defences would be reorganised and made good until the next technological advance in military destruction rendered them, in turn, redundant. These shifting military and naval needs had an important influence on the local economy and physical layout of Portsmouth and Gosport.

The Romans were the first to introduce a system of coastal defence in Britain to repel Saxon and Frankish raiders, and Portchester was one of a chain extending from the Wash to Southampton Water. After the Romans departed, in around 410, the fort was only occupied sporadically until the Normans transformed it into a grand royal castle, with the addition of a keep and inner bailey.

During the reign of King John the Cinque Ports of Dover, Hastings, Romney, Hythe and Sandwich began to silt up and Portsmouth was chosen to be a base for naval expeditions to Normandy. The upper harbour had also become impractical for use by larger ships, and docks near the mouth of the harbour were established and enclosed. Defensive earthworks protecting the town were also dug. In 1338, at the beginning of the Hundred Years War, some French galleys flying the English flag landed soldiers near Portsmouth and plundered and burned the town, the first of several attacks on Portsmouth and Gosport. In the following year a royal mandate was made for 'enclosing with walls, paving with stone, and improving our town of Portsmouth',[1] and in 1342 the Crown granted tax exemptions and the privilege of levying a toll on merchants to pay for the new defensive earthworks. However, captains of merchant vessels tended to sail on to Southampton to avoid payment of the toll. In contrast to the solid stone walls that protected Southampton, Portsmouth appears to have been enclosed by mud, timber and ditches by the end of the century.

With the revival of hostilities with France – during which Henry V sailed out of Portsmouth Harbour to fight at Agincourt – the first stone defence was constructed at the mouth of the Harbour. The Round Tower was built in *c.*1416-22, and a wooden tower on the Gosport side was finished in *c.*1426. These were the 'king's towers' from which a 'mighty chain of iron' was laid across the harbour mouth.[2] This could be raised by capstans and floats to prevent vessels entering the Harbour. Up until the Second World War there have been many different chains and booms designed to keep out potential enemies, from medieval raiding parties to 20th-century U-Boats. The Gosport tower was the precursor of Fort Blockhouse; the word 'blockhouse' meant a building which was used to block an enemy attack.

In 1494 work began on the Square Tower and a bulwark to defend the town from attack from the seaward side, and in the following year the first dry dock was started (see Chapter 4). In 1526 the town's defences were reported to be in a poor state of repair, but a Franco-Spanish invasion threat, precipitated by the quarrel between Henry VIII and the Pope, prompted an effort to strengthen the defences of the south coast. By the 1540s, castles were under construction in the Solent area at Sandown, East and West Cowes, Calshot, Netley, Southsea and Haselworth, and later at Yarmouth. Carisbrooke Castle was also totally reconstructed. A bulwark was established at Portsbridge to defend Portsea Island from the north. Much of this work was

funded by the proceeds from the Dissolution of the Monasteries. Southsea Castle is reputed to have been designed by Henry VIII personally, and was intended to cover the deep-water channel approach into the Harbour at a point where ships are brought closest to shore. It incorporated the latest Italian ideas in fortifications, with the introduction of angled bastions, offering a smaller target than traditional round towers which had become vulnerable to cannon. Several angled earthen bastions were also added to the Portsmouth defences in the 16th century. Haselworth Castle was built on a site in the Fort Gilkicker/Monckton area at Gosport to cover an attack from the west, but became redundant within a few decades.

During the reign of Queen Elizabeth, in the years leading up to the invasion attempt by the Spanish Armada, the ramparts and moats encircling the town were

2 *(top)*
Views of the Round Tower and Point Barracks (top) and the Square Tower, Saluting Battery and Grand Parade, *c.*1875.

3 *(below)*
Detail from an engraving based on a Tudor wall painting, showing Henry VIII riding towards Southsea Castle in 1545.

4 & 5
The (officers') Sally Port, viewed from within and without.

extensively remodelled and the town quay was rebuilt. The Queen instituted the first public lottery in 1569 to help finance this work and that at other ports.

Following the restoration of the monarchy in 1660, Charles II ordered a major rebuilding of the defences of the area. The King's Chief Engineer was a Dutchman, Sir Bernard de Gomme, who totally reconstructed the Portsmouth defences, enlarging the ramparts and bastions and adding four large ravelins (fortified islands in the moat). Similar work, but on a smaller scale, was carried out to enclose Gosport. The Gosport Lines were augmented by the building of Fort Charles (on the site of what is now Camper & Nicholson's) and Fort James on Burrow Island (also known as Rat Island), on the Gosport side of the Harbour, both of which were constructed in 1678-9. De Gomme also drew up plans for a Fort at Blockhouse, but construction was delayed until the 1710s. During the latter half of the 18th century, the Gosport Lines were rebuilt to enclose a large area to the north including the sites of the Royal Clarence Victualling Yard and what was later to become Priddy's Hard. Fort Monckton was built between 1782 and 1795, along with small batteries at Gilkicker Point and Browndown.[3]

De Gomme built two large batteries at Point, one of which was reconstructed in 1848-50 as Point Battery. Two Sally Ports, one for officers (next to the Square Tower), and the other for seamen and the public, provided access through to the beach from Broad Street.

The Hilsea Lines, comprised of earthen, moated ramparts, were built in 1746-7 to defend Portsea Island from a land attack from the north. The deep moat ran parallel to the creek, from Portsmouth Harbour to Langstone Harbour, and a 16th-century bastion at Portsbridge was strengthened to defend the entrance to the Island. The Hilsea Lines were reconstructed as a secondary line of defence to the Portsdown Hill forts in 1858-60, incorporating the 'Hilsea Arches' to allow traffic onto the island.

Fort Cumberland was built by the Duke of Richmond around an old farm on the extreme south-east point of Portsea Island in 1745-6, but was entirely rebuilt in 1789-94 by convict labour. Designed to defend the entrance to Langstone Harbour, and augmented by Eastney and Lumps Batteries, it was soon described as 'perfectly useless', prompting the couplet from Edward Gibbon:

> To raise this bulwark at enormous price,
> The head of folly used the hand of vice.[4]

The most important defensive works from this time were the enclosure of the Dockyard and the adjoining, growing settlement of Portsea, which was comprised largely of houses built by Dockyard workers.

An account of the fortifications, written in the early years of peace between Waterloo and the Crimean War, presents the ramparts as a good excuse for a pleasant walk, a portrait which is echoed today in the marketing of fortifications as leisure attractions:

6
Fort Cumberland, c.1907. Royal Marine Artillerymen with field guns.

7
Gun salute during a visit by Prince Albert in 1855.

A right pleasant stroll it is along these ramparts. They are open to pedestrians from end to end. Generally speaking, the line of fortification consists of a raised earthen terrace, exterior to all the streets of the town, and elevated several feet above their level. This terrace is gravelled at the top, and has in many parts rows of fine elms, which contribute eminently to its beauty as a promenade. On the outer edge of this terrace is a breast-work, or earth-work, connected with the outer fortifications, and raised four or five feet higher than the terrace. The bastions, of which there are several, are deeply embayed recesses, into which the terrace recedes further from the centre of the town. These recesses are mostly four-sided spaces of ground, surrounded by the breast work through which are pierced holes for the mouths of cannons. Without being deeply learned in military matters, we can manage to form a guess at the use of these bastions, when we stand on the terrace and see in what direction the guns point; they command the exterior fortifications on all sides; so that should an enemy gain possession of the latter, he would still have a warm reception from the defenders within. The external fortifications here spoken of consist chiefly of ravelins, which are triangular spaces of ground, where ditches, ramparts, covered ways, and the sloping glacis, spread over an immense area, and give one some foretaste of the machinery involved in the terrible art of besieging and defending a town. These fortifications are, for the most part kept in perfect order; but still the nice green sward with which most of the earth-works are covered, render the ramparts or terraces a very acceptable promenade; and when the garrison band is playing on the green in front of the governor's house, near the King's Bastion, the enlivening scene is only such as can be

8 *(above)*
Quay Gate, 1882.

9 *(below left)*
The Landport Gate, also known as
the Town Gate.

10 *(below)*
King James's Gate at the time of the
Fleet Review of 1856.

11 *(right)*
Plan of Old Portsmouth in 1910,
showing line of old fortifications.

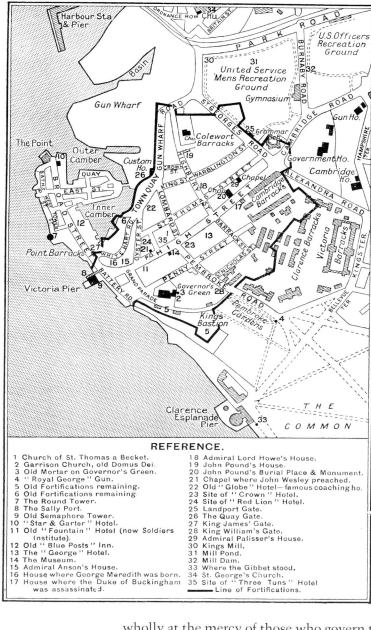

REFERENCE.

1 Church of St. Thomas a Becket.
2 Garrison Church, old Domus Dei.
3 Old Mortar on Governor's Green.
4 " Royal George " Gun.
5 Old Fortifications remaining.
6 Old Fortifications remaining.
7 The Round Tower.
8 The Sally Port.
9 Old Semaphore Tower.
10 " Star & Garter " Hotel.
11 Old " Fountain " Hotel (now Soldiers Institute).
12 Old " Blue Posts " Inn.
13 The " George " Hotel.
14 The Museum.
15 Admiral Anson's House.
16 House where George Meredith was born.
17 House where the Duke of Buckingham was assassinated.
18 Admiral Lord Howe's House.
19 John Pound's House.
20 John Pound's Burial Place & Monument.
21 Chapel where John Wesley preached.
22 Old " Globe " Hotel—famous coaching ho.
23 Site of " Crown " Hotel.
24 Site of " Red Lion " Hotel.
25 Landport Gate.
26 The Quay Gate.
27 King James' Gate.
28 King William's Gate.
29 Admiral Palisser's House.
30 Kings Mill.
31 Mill Pond.
32 Mill Dam.
33 Where the Gibbet stood.
34 St. George's Church.
35 Site of " Three Tuns " Hotel
—— Line of Fortifications.

displayed in a garrison town …

At three different points in the circuit of Portsmouth are roads cut through the ramparts by means of arch-work, and communication from the interior to the exterior. One of these is the Quay-gate [which later led to the swing bridge that separated the Outer and Inner Cambers], another the Landport-gate [formerly known as St Thomas's Gate], and a third the Spur-gate [replaced by King William's Gate in 1834; the writer has omitted King James's Gate, which stood at the end of Broad Street]; and there are two of a similar kind at Portsea, called the Lion-gate [incorporated into the Semaphore Tower in the Dockyard in 1929] and the Unicorn-gate [re-erected as an entrance to the Dockyard in 1865]. These gates and roads are so completely overlooked by lines of fortification, that the out-goers and in-comers, whether men, or horses, or vehicles, are wholly at the mercy of those who govern the ramparts for the time being. The ramparts, or terraces, pass continuously over these roads; and there are, at intervals, flights of steps, or sloping paths, to lead down from the ramparts to the streets within the town, but none to the exterior. The interior and the exterior are certainly widely different in that respect; for while the former presents a mass of streets, cooped up within limits incapable of expansion, the latter presents much liveliness and openness of view.[5]

By the mid-19th century, developments in military technology and increasing fears of France prompted a review of defences which was to change irrevocably the local landscape, and the promenading habits of visitors. With the invention of breech-loading artillery capable of firing explosive shells over twice the range of traditional cannon, the advantage was now with the aggressor. The French had started development of a fleet of steam-powered, iron-clad warships and were also building a new naval base at Cherbourg.

As well as strengthening the defences at the mouth of the Harbour (Point Battery and Fort Blockhouse) and Southsea Castle, two lines of forts were built as a defence against landward attack. These incorporated the latest ideas, the ramparts being designed to hold as many guns as possible, with bomb-proof passageways (caponiers) projecting into the moat making a polygon shape. The Gosport Advanced Line, comprised of forts Gomer, Grange, Rowner, Brockhurst and Elson, stretched from Stokes Bay, across the peninsula, to the western side of the Harbour. A second line, further west, was planned from Fareham to Lee-on-Solent, but only Fort Fareham was completed. Portsmouth's first line of defence for an attack from the north was to be a line of seven forts along the crest of Portsdown Hill, but only five were built, forts Wallington, Nelson, Southwick, Widley and Purbrook, along with Farlington and Crookhorn Redoubts in the east.

12 *(above)*
Fort Blockhouse in 1855, shortly after reconstruction.

13 *(below)*
Fort Widley, *c*.1920.

Though since ridiculed as 'Palmerston's Folly' (after the Prime Minister who advocated their building), the new forts gave reassurance to those who feared invasion. A local parish magazine defended the building of the hill forts:

It has become necessary to occupy [Portsdown Hill], since rifled ordnance has attained such a range, that an enemy,

14 *(above)*
Spit Bank Fort under construction in 1872, before the addition of 25-inch thick metal armour cladding on the north face. The entrance to Portsmouth Harbour is on the right.

15 *(right)*
No Man's Land Fort, practice gun-firing, *c.*1900.

16 *(below)*
The entrance to Portsmouth Harbour, showing Fort Blockhouse (left), *c.*1882.

who planted his batteries there, might throw shells into the dockyard, setting fire to and destroying the buildings and stores.[6]

A seaward attack from the west was anticipated by the construction of the Stokes Bay Lines, which incorporated a moat and an earthen parapet, flanked by five batteries. The Gilkicker and Browndown batteries were rebuilt to accommodate new artillery, and were part of a large battery network that included new ones at Southsea Castle, Lumps Fort and Eastney. Shore batteries were also built at the western end of the Solent at the Needles and Hurst Castle, to defend the shipping channel. The Needles Passage was considered the 'back door' to Portsmouth and Southampton, and to protect the batteries from an attack from the rear, a fort was built at Freshwater, later to be named Golden Hill Fort.

17
Searchlights from Southsea Castle and Spit Bank Fort, *c*.1913.

At the eastern end of the Solent, Sandown Bay, which only had a 17th-century fort, was considered vulnerable and a cluster of batteries was established around it, backed up by Bembridge Fort. Puckpool Mortar Battery was built near Ryde, but the eastern approach was considered too wide to be defended solely by shore batteries. The construction of a permanent barrier was considered but rejected on the grounds of cost and the potential side-effect of silting up the deep water channel. Eventually four reinforced granite sea forts were built spanning the Solent, Spit Sand (Spit Bank), Horse Sand Fort, No Man's Land (Nomansland) Fort and St Helen's Fort.

In the latter half of the 19th century, the Portsmouth area became one of the most strongly defended places in the world. But changing military technology soon rendered these fixed defences effectively obsolete. Opponents of the scheme argued that the money should have been spent on modernising the Navy, pointing out that:

An enemy, once in possession of the outer forts on Portsdown Hill, would have the Hilsea lines and Portsmouth at its mercy: so that it is marvellous any one ever conceived the idea of this inner line of forts, still less that Parliament should have sanctioned it … It is popularly said that the double line of forts has cost over £11,000,000.[7]

Though obsolete, the forts dismissed as 'Palmerston's Folly' served in the two world wars either as anti-aircraft gun and searchlight emplacements, administrative headquarters, ammunition stores, radar facilities or barracks. As

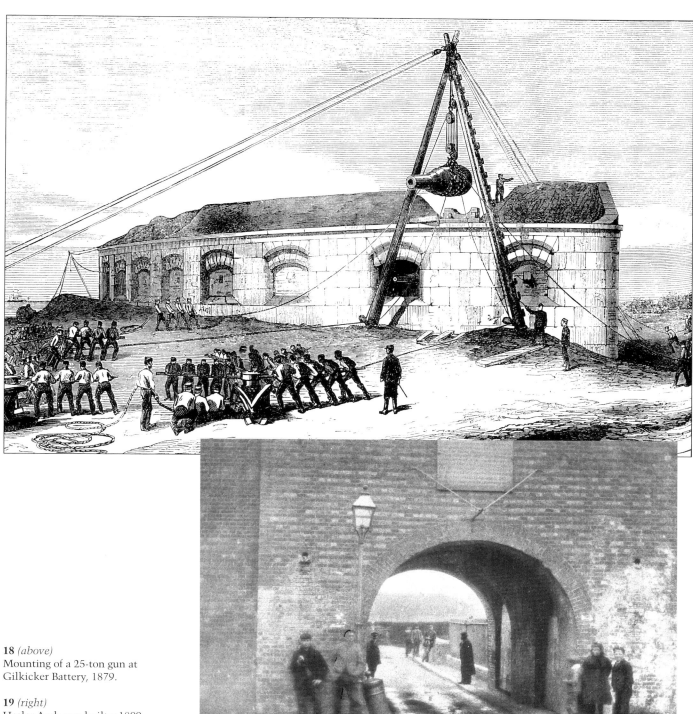

18 *(above)*
Mounting of a 25-ton gun at
Gilkicker Battery, 1879.

19 *(right)*
Haslar Arch was built *c*.1800,
providing access through the Gosport
Lines near Holy Trinity Church.

well as the harbour boom defence, other booms were built spanning the Solent,
including one stretching from Lumps Fort to Nettlestone Point on the Isle of
Wight. Barrage balloons were introduced along the coast and in other vulnerable
areas in 1939 as a hindrance to air attack. Another defensive measure against night

20 *(right)*
Southsea Castle, from an engraving dated 1783.

21 *(below)*
6-inch guns on the East Battery, Southsea Castle, *c.*1930.

22 *(bottom)*
Barrage balloon over Fratton, *c.*1940. These balloons were
intended to prevent enemy aircraft from flying at a low
level. During the Battle of Britain there were 32 in the
skies over Portsmouth, and 24 over Gosport.

bombing was a series of decoy sites that were set
up in Langstone Harbour and on Hayling Island.
Controlled from Fort Purbrook, these decoys
simulated ineffectively blacked-out areas and
sites that had been bombed and were ablaze. As
a result, the Luftwaffe harmlessly dropped
many hundreds of bombs into Langstone Harbour and sparsely populated areas of Hayling
Island.[8] The use of the decoy, a traditional military tactic as old as war itself, proved to be the
most effective protection of the 'Smitten City'
of Portsmouth during the Second World War.

Chapter 2

THE ARMY AND ITS BARRACKS

23
The first Governor's (Government) House and Domus Dei.

From around 1290 the Constable of Portchester Castle had responsibility for the military matters of 'Portesmouthe and of the Country about', though, by the beginning of the 16th century, the post had been superseded by the new office of Governor in command of a permanent garrison at Portsmouth.[1] By the 17th century a Deputy Governor's post had been established, based in Gosport. When Southsea Castle was built, in 1544, another separate and much smaller garrison was set up under a Captain.

During the Middle Ages the town and its environs was an important mustering point for fleets to transport armies to France. In 1229, Henry III assembled 'one of the finest armies that had ever been raised in England' in the locality, and in 1294 an army of 20,000 foot soldiers and 500 men-at-arms also set sail from the port. Edward III left with an army reported to be 32,000 strong in 1346, prior to his victory at Crecy, and in 1386 King Richard II saw off an expedition to Spain made up of 20,000 men-at-arms and 8,000 archers. In 1475, Edward IV reviewed his entire army of 30,000 on Froddington Heath (later Southsea Common). Henry VIII's army assembled there in preparation to repel the French attack of 1545, during which the *Mary Rose* sank. The Common was used increasingly for military encampments and training and in 1785 the land was sold by the Lord of the Manor to the Government, formalising its military role:

24
Government House 1882-1940.

By 1626, Portsmouth was described as the strongest town in the country, with a 'great garrison'; a breakdown of personnel from 1630 describes this as one master gunner, 15 gunners, one ancient, one armourer, one sergeant, one drummer, one fife, and 100 soldiers.[2] By the time of the Civil War, the garrison had been reinforced several-fold by impressment. The Governor, Colonel George Goring, attempted to hold the town for the King, but desertion was widespread and the number of troops at his disposal fell to 300. At Southsea Castle the garrison had been reduced to 12 men, and it was unable to put up any effective resistance to the Parliamentary storming party which numbered more than 400. Goring capitulated soon afterwards and the Castle was used as a military prison during the years of the Commonwealth. The Portsmouth garrison was restored under Parliament to include a master gunner, 2 gunners, 14 matrosses (artillerymen), gunsmith, 440 soldiers, and officers, and by the time of the Restoration, the annual cost of Portsmouth Garrison was £10,261, more than any other garrison in the country.[3]

A spacious and comfortable house was provided for the Governor near Domus Dei in 1658, and, four years later, King Charles II celebrated his wedding to the Duchess of Braganza in the great hall. This, and subsequent Governors' houses, became known as Government House. After demolition in 1826, the Governor moved into a house in St Thomas Street until the early 1850s, when Admiralty House was bought by the War Office to serve as the Governor's residence. This was a fine mansion in the High Street, which had previously served as the residence of the Naval Commander-in-Chief. A new Government House was built in 1882 (close to where Portsmouth University's Frewen Library stands), but was destroyed by an incendiary bomb in 1940. The nearby Ravelin House was Garrison Commander Brigadier Montgomery's residence in 1937-8, before his decisive victory over the Afrika Korps at El Alamein and his successful role in the D-Day operations.

The post of Governor was abolished in 1834, and succeeding garrison commanders held the title of Lieutenant Governor until 1903. The land adjoining the Garrison Church, Governor's Green, was used for parades, training and inspections of garrison troops and volunteers for four centuries, often watched by the local population. During times of war the military presence was appreciated for the protection it offered, but in peacetime attitudes varied from resigned tolerance to naked hostility. One constant, however, was shock at the sight of those returning from war. During the Napoleonic Wars, a returning rifleman, Benjamin Harris, noted,

> the inhabitants of Portsmouth, who had assembled in some numbers to see us land, were horror-stricken that their countrymen, and their relatives, were returning to England in such a ghastly state.[4]

During the First World War the same horrified reaction met the hundreds of limbless and blinded soldiers who were deposited on platform 2 of Fratton Railway Station *en route* to a temporary hospital in Fawcett Road.

While death and injury does not respect rank, the Governor's traditional lifestyle and living conditions contrasted starkly with the men under his command. In 1630 his annual salary was around £180 while a gunner received about £10. By the 1730s, he enjoyed a salary of £700 while the cost of the wages of the entire garrison was £2,000.

Before barracks were established in the town, soldiers were lodged in the cold and spartan towers and gates of the fortifications, or were billeted on publicans or

25
Brigadier B.L. Montgomery served as Garrison Commander in 1937-8.

in inhabitants' hovels. This imposition on ordinary townsfolk was deeply resented, but refusal to accept resulted in an appearance before the Borough Justices. A rapid expansion of the armed forces during the brief reign of James II exacerbated the situation. The number of soldiers was doubled to nearly 1,500 and the sharing of beds was encouraged by the military authorities. Grievances continued despite an increase in the accommodation rate payable to householders as an incentive.

In 1689 the municipal authorities raised a petition, complaining that the citizens had

> suffered much by soldiers left behind their colours, by their wives and
> children when they die or march, by debts they contract beyond their
> pay, but particularly by the great disorders lately committed by the Irish,
> who not only made themselves masters of the houses by free quartering
> but threatened to destroy the petitioners which it is believed they would
> have done.[5]

On at least one occasion, tensions appear to have led to serious public disorder. Further complaints were made to the Secretary of War by the Mayor about the continued practice of billeting bills being left unpaid. Implicit in the petitions and complaints was the need for the provision of permanent barracks. This ran counter to the attitude of Parliament, which objected strongly to the establishment of barracks anywhere because it implied approval of an expensive standing army. The view was that if soldiers were set up in barracks there would be no incentive to disband them when hostilities or the threat of war had ended. Consequently, for many years, the number of commissions for new barracks bore little relationship to the need in places like Portsmouth.

Colewort or New Barracks, situated at the north end of St Mary's Street (now Highbury Street), is said to have been the first permanent barracks in the country, having been converted from the first military hospital in the town a few years after its construction in 1680. Inevitably, the accommodation was insufficient to meet the shifting needs of the military, and billeting continued in public houses, and, on a smaller scale, in private residences. In 1745, Colewort Barracks had 144 beds, though this was increased three-fold after the demolition of neighbouring houses freed up land for an extension in the 1820s. In 1860 a public right of way through the barracks was abolished because of the opportunities it presented for soldiers to indulge in immoral practices.

In the late 1720s, the garrison was said to be comprised of four hundred men in peacetime, but was increased to two regiments of foot in wartime. Members of the garrison were 'invalids' (soldiers unfit for foreign service) and were known as 'old fogeys' by the local population, giving some idea of the regard in which they were generally held. Many lived in a group of houses in St Nicholas Street known as 'Fourhouse Barracks' because of the four royal brewing houses that had occupied the site in medieval times. The doors to these houses were so low that 'it used to be an amusement to the local populace to see (them) in their enormous cocked hats emerge from their inhabitations'.[6] These buildings were demolished in about

1770 and the purpose-built Fourhouse Barracks erected in their place (later to become part of Old Clarence Barracks).

In a humorous account of the Borough published in 1748, Robert Wilkins commented on the relationship between the military and local residents:

> The Military Gentlemen also keep themselves a distinct People, and never care to herd with us Townsfolk: but this is easily accounted for, as they are generally well bred Men, who cannot bear Rusticity, and brutal Ill-Manners. We endeavour tho' to be remiss as they in cultivating a Correspondence; not because they shew that Contempt for us we perhaps deserve, but for their professing to know us too well, to be over-reached by us; for their extreme Parsimony and Unwillingness to increase our Stock. Soldiers make their fortunes with Danger and Difficulty, and spend them with Caution; especially the graver Sort, of which ours chiefly consist.[7]

During wartime, civil authority gave way to the military, and the Governor took effective control of the town, but in peacetime there were considerable tensions when interests conflicted. The construction or demolition of buildings by the military and the non-payment of local tolls and rent were two complaints made to the Lord Treasurer of England by local burgesses during the governorship of Sir Adrian Poynings (1559-71). Poynings appears to have been a temperamental character who was a law unto himself.[8] In 1557 he personally took part in a violent raid on a burgess and future mayor, John Holloway, and attempted to abduct his wife. Colonel George Goring (1639-42) had a similar, cavalier disregard for the rights of the townspeople, and Colonel Sir John Gibson (1701-2) threatened to turn guns of garrison upon Dockyard shipwrights if they dared to build dwelling houses at Portsea. Gibson was also notorious for the harsh punishments he meted out to soldiers who breached military discipline. Many were tortured astride a rigid frame called the 'wooden horse' with weighty objects tied to each leg. A more traditional punishment in both the army and navy was whipping, though local people did not always approve of such barbarity. In 1796 a soldier who was accused of attempting to strike an officer was sentenced to 300 lashes, a punishment that could sometimes prove fatal. It was claimed that he had only tried to defend himself against an officer and a sergeant. Large groups of local people turned out to hiss and throw stones at officers of the Bucks militia. The last flogging of a British soldier was said to have taken place at the Artillery Barracks before corporal punishment was formally abolished by the Army in 1881.

An account of the execution of a soldier on Portsdown Hill in 1803 is given by Private Benjamin Harris of the 66th Regiment of Foot, who was picked as a member of the firing party. Harris estimated that 15,000 men from the area were assembled to witness the execution. The man had been found guilty of persistently enlisting and deserting, acquiring 16 King's shillings in the process.

> After being blindfolded, he was desired to kneel down behind a coffin, which had been placed on the ground. The drum-major of the Hilsea depot gave us an expressive glance, and we immediately commenced

loading. This was done in the deepest silence. The next moment we were primed and ready. There was a dreadful pause for a few moments, then the drum-major, again looking towards us, gave the signal before agreed upon – a flourish of his cane – and we levelled and fired. We had been strictly enjoined to be steady and take good aim, and the poor fellow, pierced by several balls, fell heavily upon his back.[9]

Harris describes how the dying man was finished off by four shots into the head, and how the assembled soldiers were ordered to march past the corpse, company by company, in slow time.

In 1840, in contrast to the generally harsh treatment of ordinary soldiers, officers who had stolen an expensive pair of pistols and vandalised several business in the town were ordered only to pay the cost of the damage. The editor of the *Hampshire Telegraph* called for the resignation of the Lieutenant-Governor, Sir Hercules Pakenham. The local press also sympathised with soldiers of the 77th Regiment (Atholl Highlanders) in 1783 when they mutinied after discovering that their officers had sold them to the East India Company to protect business interests in India.

26
Grand Parade with Main Guard House on the left, and military memorial cross (8th King's Regiment).

Duelling, though illegal, was practised on numerous occasions by officers from all three armed services in the Portsmouth area. It was seen as a gentleman's means of vindicating his honour, and the law turned a blind eye whenever it proved fatal. In the first few years of the 19th century, fatal duels are recorded at Fort Monckton (1801), Southsea Common (1812), behind a pub in Broad Street (1800), Gosport (1807). The last fatal duel in the country took place at Browndown in 1845 when a soldier, Captain Alexander Seton of the 11th Dragoons, died of his wounds after paying attention to the wife of a Royal Marine.

The town's Main Guard House was on the Grand Parade near the Platform Battery, and was erected in the reign of George III. There were also Guard Houses associated with the town gates and Mill Redoubt, which were often used to hold drunken soldiers, or those who had broken leave. Southsea Castle was used, once again, as a military prison after the barrack rooms were converted to accommodate 150 military prisoners in 1844, though a gunner from the Royal Artillery was retained as a reminder of its defensive function. Prisoners were transferred to the newly built Forton Military Prison in Lees Lane, Gosport in 1850.

The military authorities were also responsible for guarding prisoners of war. Many thousands were incarcerated, from the Dutch War of 1665 onwards, in Portchester Castle, and later in Forton Prison and convict hulks in the Harbour. During the Revolutionary Wars, there were over 10,000 in the Portsmouth area. By 1813 there were 9,000 in the hulks, 5,000 at Portchester and 4,000 at Forton. There were many ingenious attempts to escape, and the logistics of guarding, feeding and recapturing the slippery Dutch, French and American prisoners of war can only be imagined.

By the 1720s the relationship between the military and civil government had seemingly improved, as recorded by Daniel Defoe, who also noted the tolerance of local people to the daily inconveniences of living in a garrison town, a tolerance born of economic necessity:

> The Inhabitants … necessarily submit to … being Examin'd at the
> Gates, such as being obliged to keep Garrison Hours, and not be let out,
> or let in after Nine a Clock at Night, and the like; but these are Things
> no People will count a Burthen, where they get their Bread by the very
> Situation of the Place, as is the case here.[10]

This tolerance evidently did not last long. Another policing activity taken on by the army in the 1740s was the capture of navy deserters. Local sympathies tended to be with the seamen, and every means of obstructing the soldiers in their duty was exercised. After being threatened while attempting to search some wagons in Portsmouth in 1745, a Captain Bagshawe complained that he needed protection from the 'lawless ruffians' who had threatened to 'have his head broke' and 'shake him out of (his) laced cloaths'.[11]

Despite ancient rules, some members of the garrison acquired burgess rights, inviting accusations of a conflict of interest. The two worlds also met in the shape of the Volunteer, a civilian who was prepared to take up part-time duties to defend the town during wartime when invasion was a possibility. Amid fears of a Spanish invasion in the 1580s, Governor Sir Henry Radcliffe (Earl of Sussex) felt the garrison of 60 men under his command was inadequate, prompting him to assist personally in the training of a volunteer force, a review of which took place at Hilsea. His returns for 1587 record 102 such volunteers from Gosport and Alverstoke, including nine with firearms, three archers and ninety bilmen (men with blades on the end of shafts). It was proposed that these men should be part of an army of 700 men, drawn from Alton, Fawley and the Portsmouth area, to defend the coast from Portsmouth to Southampton. Four hundred men were to defend the

27 *(far left)*
A 'Portsea Peacock' of 1799.

28
The Connaught Drill Hall, Gosport,
*c.*1905. Built in 1902, the hall stood
on the site of the current public
library.

vulnerable areas at Browndown and Stokes Bay, but in the event, the Spanish Armada sailed passed the Isle of Wight, and the volunteers were able to return to their trades.

During the Napoleonic Wars a number of volunteer corps were established, most conspicuously the Portsea Loyal Independent Volunteers. Officers were known as 'the Portsea Peacocks', though the corps became generally known as 'the Golden Goldfinches' because of their adornments of gold rosettes, wings and trimmings attached to a scarlet coat, under which a frilled shirt complemented blue pantaloons. Beneath a gay plumage of bear fur and white feather, their hair was frizzed and powdered. More practically, an Artillery Corps was formed from men of the Gunwharf, Victualling and Customs Departments. They carried out duties of the garrison, which numbered about two hundred in peacetime, when needed.

In 1801 at least 17 volunteer groups drawn from Portsmouth, Gosport, Havant, Emsworth, Finchdean and Petersfield took part in a grand review on Portsdown Hill, forming a line over two miles long. Several months later many other residents enrolled to fight to defend their town from the French, whose imminent arrival had been mistakenly heralded by burning beacons.

The volunteer movement was disbanded when hostilities ended, but revived again in 1847 when over a thousand Dockyard workers were armed and trained to defend the port. In 1860 a number of volunteer corps were formed including the 3rd Hampshire Volunteers and the 2nd Hampshire Volunteer Artillery. Training took place in halls in Penny Street, Hampshire Terrace, Alfred Road, Grigg Street (now St Paul's Road) and later in the Drill Hall in Stanhope Road which was opened in 1901. Between 1853 and 1894, artillery volunteers were also trained in Forts Brockhurst, Gomer and Elson. On the outbreak of the First World War the Portsmouth Volunteer Training Corps or Town Guard was set up for men who were too young, too old, or medically unfit for the regular army. Within a year, the Corps had 300 men in its ranks, while Gosport Guard, which drilled in the Connaught Drill Hall (on the site of the current public library), had around a hundred. Before the introduction of conscription in 1916, over two hundred trained Portsmouth volunteers had gone on to enlist in the army.[12] The numbers of volunteers was maintained by the military tribunals, which made exemptions from military service for those in reserved occupations conditional on regular attendance for drilling. In the Second World War, following the retreat from Dunkirk in 1940 and at a time when invasion seemed imminent, a national appeal was made for the formation of Local Defence Volunteer Corps, later to be renamed the Home Guard. Like their predecessors, they took part in anti-invasion exercises and drilled in local halls.

The tradition of Portsmouth as an embarkation point for armies continued into the 19th century, though, by then, families arrived in large numbers to see them off. In 1800, 10,000 troops, many from Ireland, left from Portsmouth and

Southampton, leaving many distraught wives and children behind in the town. The Governor, General Whitelocke, gave the families permission to sleep in Southsea Castle until a ship could be arranged to take them back to Ireland. The departure of the Baltic Fleet in 1854 was equally emotional, as described by the *Illustrated London News*:

> [The 2nd Battalion of the Rifle Brigade] left their barracks for the Dockyard, being accompanied by their own band, and the bands of other regiments in garrison. A large number of persons had assembled, and gave the troops hearty cheers … A circumstance of a romantic character occurred on the corps embarking. The wife of a private being prevented going out by the regulations of the service, she dressed herself in Rifle costume, and, gun in hand, actually marched into the Dockyard. She was, however, detected on getting on board; but we hear that permission to go out with her husband was granted to her.[13]

Thousands of troops passed through the port to take part in what was later generally regarded to be a futile and bloody war. The men were condemned to fight a winter campaign in the Crimea without proper equipment or clothing, while many families were left poorly provided for. The demand for assistance from the local Board of Guardians led to the Government eventually agreeing, in 1860, to contribute to the poor rates.

Between 1745 and 1861, army barrack accommodation in the town increased from 380 to nearly 5,000 beds. Construction and maintenance was an important

29 *(left)*
Embarkation of the Rifle Brigade for the Crimea aboard the *Vulcan*, Portsmouth Dockyard, 1854.

30 *(right)*
A troopship enters Portsmouth Harbour, laden with soldiers from the Crimea, 1856.

31 *(below)*
Returning troops prepare to disembark at Portsmouth Dockyard, 1856.

32 *(below right)*
Cambridge Barracks.

responsibility of the Royal Engineers (whose Milldam Barracks were off Lion Terrace), though local convict labour was used extensively to do the physical work. Among their many other roles was the clearing of wrecks from the seaways, and one of their proud claims was the destruction of the remains of the *Mary Rose* off Spithead in 1843.[14] Milldam House served as offices for the Engineers, was converted into a military hospital in the Second World War and, since 1993, has served as Portsmouth Register Office.

The Sappers' and Miners' barracks was situated in Commercial Road area (near Allders) but sold by the Ordnance Board in 1834 and subsequently demolished. In 1856 the Corps was absorbed by the Royal Engineers.

Clarence Barracks (of which Fourhouse Barracks formed the left wing) was rebuilt twice, in the 1770s and 1820s, and by the 1870s could accommodate several thousand men. In 1891-3 it was enlarged again, incorporating pavilions rather than blocks, and including larger, lighter and airier barrack rooms. The northern block was retained and converted into the City Museum and Art Gallery in 1972. The adjoining Cambridge Barracks (taken

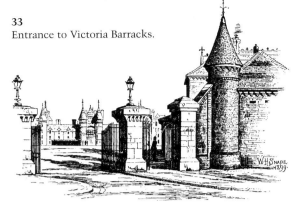

33
Entrance to Victoria Barracks.

34 *(left)*
Royal Scots Fusiliers at Clarence Barracks, 1926.

35 *(below left)*
Plan of Anglesea Barracks.

36 *(below)*
Victoria Barracks, *c.*1910.

37 *(right)*
Presentation of new Colours to the 1st Battalion Hampshire Regiment on 29 June 1907. The building on the left is the northern block of Clarence Barracks (now the City Museum).

38 *(below right)*
Heroes of the First World War receiving medals in 1917. Victoria Barracks is in the background.

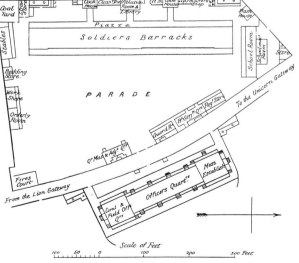

PRESENTATION OF NEW COLOURS TO 1ST HANTS REGT
BY H.R.H. PRINCESS HENRY OF BATTENBERG

HEROES DECORATED JUNE 2 1917

PRIVATE WHITE 3/R BERKS
RECEIVING THE MILITARY MEDAL
FROM MAG. GEN. HEATH CALDWELL. C.B.

39 *(right)*
New (later St George) Barracks, Gosport, *c.*1910.

40 *(centre)*
Royal Scots Fusiliers at New Barracks, Gosport, at the outbreak of the First World War, August 1914.

41 *(below left)*
No. 18 Squad, 3rd Battalion Hampshire Regiment, New Barracks, Gosport, 1918 (including a black recruit).

42 *(below right)*
St George Barracks, Gosport, 1991.

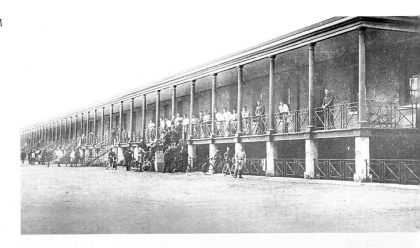

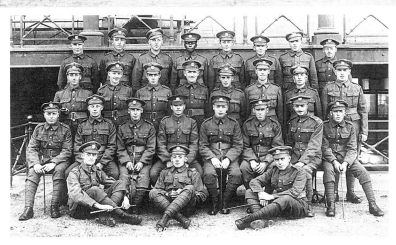

over in 1926 by Portsmouth Grammar School) originated in 1825 when some army victualling offices at the upper end of Penny Street were converted into barracks by the Royal Engineers. These were greatly extended in the 1850s and, in 1861, held 1,038 men. During the Crimean War they were used to accommodate the wives and children of men who were away fighting.

The Victoria Barracks were built in the early 1880s on the eastern side of the large military area (facing Jubilee and King's Terraces). Before being sold for redevelopment in the 1960s, it was used as a naval training school.

Anglesea Barracks was built in 1847-9 to accommodate 100 men. The soldiers' barrack block was of a modern design, divided into 53 barrack rooms, each intended for 18 men. Unlike the Officers' Quarters, this block was retained when the Naval Barracks were built on the site between 1899 and 1903.

Point Battery Barracks were built in 1847-8 after 19 Broad Street premises were bought and demolished, including the *Blue Anchor* public house, where the mutiny at Spithead is said to have been planned. New heavy guns were installed to guard the Harbour and, in 1861, a complement of 80 men is recorded. The officers' quarters and other buildings were demolished in the early 1960s, but part of the soldiers' quarters survives (and is used today by local artists to display their work).

43 *(top, middle, bottom)*
Soldiers at Fort Rowner, Gosport, *c*.1910.

In the 18th-century barrack huts were used by the army at Hilsea on the site of the Priory of Gatcombe. These were enlarged in 1794 but demolished by the end of the Napoleonic Wars in 1815. The Royal Artillery Barracks in Hilsea was built in 1854 and housed 400 men in 1861. In 1888 a garrison church was built north of the barracks and dedicated to St Barbara, the Patron Saint of Artillerists, who also gave her name to the Navy's gunnery school's church in 1934. The Royal Field Artillery was moved to Fareham in 1921 when the site became the principal Ordnance Depot for the area. The military left in the early 1960s, and the Gatcombe Park estate was built on the site.

44 *(top left)*
6th Hants leaving Portsmouth, 1914.

45 *(above)*
'Tommy's Arrival', 1909.

46 *(left)*
Demobilisation Parade, Gosport, c.1919.

47 *(right)*
Men about to be discharged at Fort Brockhurst, c.1919.

In the 18th century, Royal Artillery officers were accommodated in a group of houses in the Old Gunwharf which became known as 'The Barracks', though the Gunwharf Barracks proper were built on the south side of the New Gunwharf in the early 19th century. The Royal Marine Artillery moved in 1824, later transferring to Fort Cumberland and Eastney Barracks in the 1860s. In 1891, the Gunwharf authorities took over the barracks to store military equipment.

In Gosport, Haslar Barracks was built on a site south-west of Haslar Hospital in 1801. It was rebuilt in 1864, some of the buildings from this period having been retained to serve as a Detention Centre.

Forton Barracks was completed in 1807 and housed infantrymen and artillerymen who manned the town's fortifications and guarded the shoreline from Fort Blockhouse to Stokes Bay. After the Napoleonic Wars, they were used as transit barracks for troops, together with temporary camps on Browndown. In 1848, the army exchanged Forton Barracks for the Old Clarence Barracks in Portsmouth, and the Royal Marine Light Infantry moved in. Despite this, Forton continued to be used by the army into the 1850s.

The Gosport Barracks were built between 1856-9 with room for over 2,000 men. In the early 1860s a military hospital was added, serving the many garrison units that were based there. During the First World War, the 3rd Battalion of the Hampshire Regiment occupied the barracks for training and also for the 'rehabilitation' of the wounded before being sent back to the front. From 1890 to the Second World War, they became known as New Barracks, but from 1940-7 the Admiralty took them over for New Entry Training and the establishment was commissioned as *St George*. When the barracks were returned to the military they became known as St George (or St George's) Barracks. Like most obsolete fortifications, Fort Brockhurst served as barracks for different regiments, but during the 1900s it was a depot for men who had completed their term of service. Reservists were medically examined, kitted out for civilian life and given help finding employment.[15] This role was revived to cope with demobilisation at the end of the First World War.

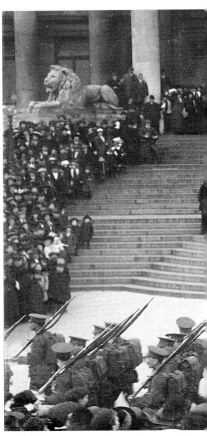

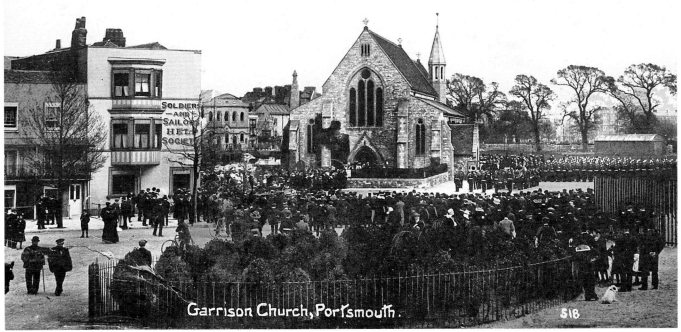

Garrison Church, Portsmouth.

48 *(far left)*
Royal Garrison Artillery postcard showing the Garrison Church, Spitbank Fort, troops in camp and on Southsea Common, *c.*1910.

49 *(below left)*
Royal Garrison Church Parade, *c.*1905.

50 *(left)*
The first Portsmouth Battalion to be recruited during the First World War march past in Town Hall Square, April 1915.

51 *(below)*
Mock-up of trenches in Town Hall Square, 1918.

52 *(bottom)*
A tank was presented to Gosport shortly after the First World War and was on display for many years in Gosport Park.

On the outbreak of war great efforts were made to persuade local men to join the Army, a task that was especially difficult in a town with a strong naval heritage. Nevertheless, before conscription was introduced in 1916, Portsmouth raised three battalions of men, each 1,100 strong. Local barracks, billeting and the Palmerston forts were inadequate to cope with the massive military presence in the area, which numbered between 25,000 and 50,000 soldiers. Sprawling camps sprung up at Hilsea and on the slopes of Portsdown Hill. These scenes were repeated during the Second World War when the American Army occupied Hilsea Barracks and nearby fields. The majority of Allied troops taking part in the D-Day operations sailed from the Hampshire coast, and, continuing the tradition dating back to the Middle Ages, Portsmouth was a major embarkation point.

53
Artillery Reservists at Portsmouth,
c.1900.

54
Preparations for D-Day in
Portsmouth Harbour, 1944.

The garrison in Portsmouth was run down in the immediate post-war years and abolished in 1960 after a presence in the area of nearly 700 years. The most senior army officer in the area was now based at St George Barracks in Gosport, but these barracks, in turn, become redundant by the early 1990s and were the subject of plans for redevelopment by the end of the century. Amid the sell-off of former Ministry of Defence land, Fort Monckton has been retained, allegedly as a military intelligence training base where MI6 officers undertake small arms training and courses in methods of espionage.[16]

Chapter 3

SEA SOLDIERS – THE ROYAL MARINES

55
The first Marine Barracks at
Portsmouth.

The first marines arrived in Portsmouth in 1668, four years after the formation of this hybrid role of 'sea soldier' and at a time when a squadron of Dutch ships was threatening the town and other points along the south coast. The Dutch wars prompted a massive increase in local ship building and repair, and provided the new marine corps, known as the 'Admiral's Regiment', with its first opportunity to win battle honours and establish itself as a force to be reckoned with. The 'sea soldiers' played a major role in the capture of Gibraltar in 1704 and were left as a garrison, bearing the brunt of Spanish attempts to recapture it.

Recruited largely in London, the first marines to be based in Portsmouth were billeted in local ale and gin houses and stables, and were later moved to Hilsea. It was not until around 1765 that the first real marine barracks was established in a converted old brewery and cooperage in St Nicholas Street. Previously known as Fourhouse Barracks it was later to be named (Old) Clarence Barracks after the Duke of Clarence. It was at about this time that the first permanent marines' band was formed.

By 1783 the men were doing garrison duty in the Dockyard, and their status in establishment circles increased during the Spithead Mutinies of 1797 when they remained loyal to their officers. This was in the face of widespread disaffection amongst naval seamen, backed by the local population. But there was also a perception that marines were rather rough types. General Wolfe considered them 'dirty, drunken, insolent rascals', though his French adversaries described what they called 'les petits grenadiers' as the most fearsome fighters they had encountered.

Throughout the 18th century, their role in action appears to have been confined to the use of small arms, and it was Lord Nelson who initiated the training of marines as artillerymen, to replace army gunners who had been used on his ships. Formed in 1804 as a separate branch, the Royal Marine Artillery (RMA) became known as the Blue Marines, from the colour of their uniform, as distinct from the

56 *(left)*
Main Gate, Forton Barracks.

57 *(right)*
Royal Marine Light Infantrymen on
the Parade Ground at Forton, *c*.1914.

58 *(below)*
Church Parade at Forton, *c*.1909.

59 *(far right)*
Gun Drill at Forton Barracks, loading
a 9.2 inch gun.

Red Marines, the Royal Marine Light Infantry (RMLI). The RMA first came to the
Portsmouth area in 1817, and were initially stationed at Fort Cumberland, then
moved to Fort Monckton, before being established in barracks in the Gunwharf in
1824. A headquarters was also set up in a house in the High Street and additional
messrooms erected in the garden.[1] There was another brief sojourn at Fort
Cumberland before Eastney Barracks was purpose-built in the 1860s. Fort
Cumberland was retained for gunnery instruction, artillery drill and bridge and
trestle building.

In 1848 the Admiralty and the Army agreed to exchange the Old Clarence
Barracks for Forton Barracks in Gosport, a move said to have been prompted by
Governor Lord Fitzclarence's frustration at not being able use the marines in the

military displays in Portsmouth in which he took great pride. The arrival of the RMLI was the most important factor in the expansion of what had previously been the rural hamlet of Forton, with a school, swimming pool, gymnasium, concert room, canteen and theatre being added to the barracks. Not unconnected with this influx of marines was the establishment of several public houses and a home for 'friendless and fallen girls' in Forton Road. Forton developed into the main depot for the training of musketry, with annual contests taking place on the ranges at Browndown.

The sheds at Forton housed guns and gun ports that were fitted out, as far as possible, like a man-of-war. One gun was mounted on a rolling-motion platform, simulating conditions at sea. Maxim machine-gun practice, using blanks, took place over Forton Creek while the use of live ammunition was safely confined to a RM launch at Spithead. Trainee buglers were sent to practice in a remote area behind the barracks that had once been used as a burial ground.[2]

Marines of the best physique were often selected for the RMA and trained at Eastney for two years in naval gun drill, field battery, garrison and siege drills, and musketry and infantry drills. Officers received the same training, after having first attended the Royal Naval College at Woolwich, a naval gunnery course at *Excellent* and a torpedo course at *Vernon*.

Officers and men of the Marine Corps were attached to one of three divisions, Portsmouth, Plymouth or Chatham, throughout their period of service, and were 'detached' from their division for service at sea. Apart from manning the guns and being prepared to land at a moment's notice, duties included acting as officers' servants, sentry duty, and, traditionally, acting as the ship's bugler, postman, barber, butcher and lamp-trimmer.

The basic accommodation at Eastney Barracks was completed in 1867, though the programme of building continued for another 40 years. The six-storey landmark water-tower, built in 1870-71, was later converted to a clock-tower utilising the old Woolwich Dockyard clock. Like Forton, Eastney Barracks developed its own community with a church, library, canteen, billiard

60 *(below)*
This Royal Marine Band, seen here at Whale Island, *c.*1914, was drafted to HMS *Bulwark* on the outbreak of the First World War. The band was playing when there was an accident in the cordite store and *Bulwark* blew up. Of the 800 crew, only 12 survived.

rooms, swimming baths, gymnasium and theatre. By 1871, the Eastney area was dominated by the Royal Marines, with over 850 servicemen in the barracks, and over 300 living in the rapidly developing surrounding area.

The RMA Divisional Band was formed in 1861, and was chosen by Edward VII to become the permanent Royal Yacht band in 1904, causing consternation at Gosport where the RMLI band had been the favourite of Queen Victoria and accompanied her on many cruises. These rival bands attended ceremonial functions and were very popular attractions in their respective communities, especially the weekly spectacle of church parade when residents lined the streets to enjoy the uplifting,

61 *(left)*
Changing the Guard at Forton Barracks, *c.*1920.

62 *(top)*
Officers' Mess at Forton, *c.*1910.

63 *(above)*
Marines at Browndown, Gosport,

*c.*1909. Routine manoeuvres and annual musketry contests were held on the ranges here between rival divisions.

64 *(right)*
Eastney Barracks Main Entrance and Clock/Water Tower.

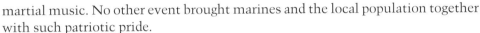

martial music. No other event brought marines and the local population together with such patriotic pride.

Separate from these bands, the Royal Naval School of Music was established at Eastney in 1903 to train boys for ships' bands. Within ten years, 53 bands had been fully trained. In 1930 the school moved to Deal, though the Portsmouth band remained at Eastney until its closure in 1991. The Royal Marines Band Service is now established in the former Royal Naval Detention Quarters at *Nelson*.[3]

While visiting Eastney Barracks in 1890, Kaiser Wilhelm remarked that 'The British Marine is the best all-round fighting man in the world', a compliment that the Royal Marines did their best to live up to in the First World War. The majority of Eastney's marines served as part of the Royal Naval Brigade and saw action in Gallipoli and on the Western Front. Many were lost in action at sea in the Battle of Jutland in 1916.

65 *(above left)*
Survivors of the Zeebrugge Raid return to Forton Barracks in April 1918.

66 *(below left)*
RMLI Ammunition Instruction.

67 *(below)*
Boat's crew of RM Artillerymen, c.1897.

68 *(above)*
Trestle building at Fort Cumberland.

69 *(above right)*
RM Artillerymen at Fort
Cumberland with 12 pr. field gun.

70 *(below)*
Officers' Quarters, Eastney Barracks.

Men of the Portsmouth Division also took part in the daring Zeebrugge Raid of 1918, when one man in two was either killed, wounded or taken prisoner. The RMLI band led survivors back to barracks at Forton where they were given a hero's welcome.

In 1923 the rival RMA and RMLI were amalgamated and Forton Barracks closed, Eastney becoming the Portsmouth Division headquarters. The Second World War saw expansion, with a camp of huts being built in Henderson Road to accommodate new recruits. Known initially as Hutment Camp, the name was changed to Melville Camp, and later Cammachio Camp, before demolition in

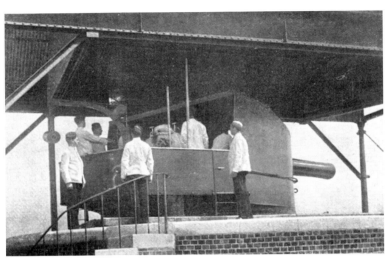

71 *(left)*
RMA gun drill at Eastney with 9.2 inch gun.

72 *(below left)*
A barrack room at Eastney, *c.*1910.

73 *(below)*
The Marine's pet dog, Nell, at Eastney, 1884.

74 *(right)*
RMA King's Bodyguard in front of Long Barracks, *c.*1914.

75 *(below right)*
Putting theory into practice – Artillerymen afloat with their guns.

1976. Cockleshell Gardens was built on the site to commemorate the heroic mission of ten men who set off up the River Gironde in canoes, or 'cockleshells', to fix limpet mines to enemy shipping in Bordeaux Harbour.

The training of Commando units had passed exclusively from the Army to the Marines by the end of the war, and with post-war defence cuts and the decline in sea service it was this role that the Corps embraced, with Eastney taking on a reduced, increasingly administrative function. Fort Cumberland became the home of the Amphibious School, which built on the experience of the 'cockleshell heroes' and trained men in water-based, clandestine activities until 1954, when it was transferred to Poole. However, the Special Boat Service, as it was renamed, continues to train in the Portsmouth Harbour and Solent area, and also uses the Navy's diving centre on Horsea Island.

The Technical and Signals Training Wings also relocated to Poole in the early 1970s. Eastney Barracks closed in 1991, marking the end of over three centuries of the marine's colourful and popular presence on Portsea Island. Some administrative functions were transferred from Eastney, Plymouth and London to a new headquarters on the west side of Whale Island.

76 *(above)*
Marine writing a letter home from Eastney Barracks during manoeuvres, 1884.

77 *(top right)*
RMA 12-inch gun turret class at Eastney.

78 *(middle right)*
Anti-torpedo boat gun drill at Eastney.

79 *(bottom right)*
Drill shed at Eastney Barracks, *c*.1916. The barrack rooms are on the right and the recreation and washrooms on the left.

80 *(above left)*
Artillerymen at Fort Cumberland.

81 *(left)*
The Gymnasium at Eastney Barracks.

82 *(above)*
RMA swimming baths at Eastney.

83 *(below left)*
The RMA Church, St Andrew's,
c.1910.

84 *(below)*
The Crinoline Church, which was
originally built as a hospital in the
Crimea, ended its days serving the
RMA at Eastney until St Andrew's
was built in 1905.

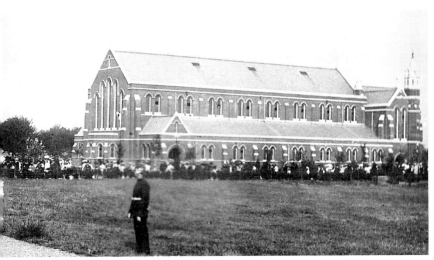

Chapter 4

THE DOCKYARD

85
Main Dockyard Gate, *c.*1899.

The natural harbour of Portsmouth has been used as a point of departure and a rendezvous for fleets since at least Roman times when they had their stronghold at Portchester and named it *Portus Magnus*. It is reasonable to suppose that *ad hoc* means of building and maintaining boats have been in existence in the area since at least that time, though it was not until the 13th century that a distinctive dockyard was established.

In 1194 King Richard I ordered a dock to be built at Portsmouth in preparation for using the area as an assembly point for attacks on the French. His successor, King John, formalised the arrangement in 1212 by ordering that the docks (at the entrance to the Mill Pond, on the site of the current Gunwharf development) be enclosed with a 'good and strong wall … for the preservation of our ships and galleys', and that storehouses be built for ships' tackle.[1] This work was carried out by the Archdeacon of Taunton, William of Wrotham, who held the office of Keeper of the King's Ships. It was during John's reign that Portsmouth became a principal naval port, superseding the Cinque Ports which had become too small to accommodate the fleet.

For much of the 15th century the River Hamble was preferred for the repair and cleaning of ships, where they were floated onto mudflats or drawn up on shore to enable work to be carried out below the water line. A dramatic increase in the size of ships made this increasingly difficult. The ships were too heavy to be hauled ashore and the Hamble became too shallow to accommodate them. And so, in 1495, Henry VII ordered the construction of the country's first dry dock by the deep waters of Portsmouth Harbour (near to where HMS *Victory* is currently preserved). It took nearly a year to build and included two sets of wooden gates and a horse-driven 'ingyn to draw water owte'. The space between the gates was filled with clay and gravel to help prevent water re-entering the dock. A storehouse, smithy and forge were also built, the total cost being £193 0s. 5d. and three farthings.

The first ship known to have used the dock was the *Sovereign*, a 600-ton vessel that required 140 men to carry out the docking process. When she left eight months later it took 20 men nearly a month to clear the way through the gates. These early dockyard workers received set rates of pay according to their skills, and included caulkers, smiths, surveyors, carpenters, sawyers, shipwrights, carters and labourers.

The first named ship to be built at Portsmouth was the *Sweepstake* in 1497, though many others had been launched without ceremony before that date. The King's shipwrights were sent into the Forest of Bere and the New Forest to fell and prepare timber for his ships. The ill-fated *Mary Rose*, named after Henry VIII's sister, was one of the solid oak and elm ships built in the 1500s.

The establishment of a permanent navy and the increase in the number and size of Henry VIII's ships during the wars with France led to a corresponding increase in the number of workshops and storehouses. In 1514 the first Keeper of the Storehouses, John Hopton, was appointed, a post that was to become, in effect, the paymaster of the navy. Though Henry VIII has been regarded, traditionally, as the founder of the Royal Navy (despite the fact that, as we have seen, some medieval kings maintained fleets), his lasting achievement was to establish a permanent administration ashore which made a permanent fleet possible and sustainable.

In 1527, nine acres of waterside land was purchased for £9 to extend the Yard. A ditch was dug and a hedge planted around the perimeter and gates installed to allow access to the growing army of workmen. Some idea of the logistics involved in docking a ship is given in an account of repairs on the *Henri Grace a Dieu*, when an estimated 1,000 men were employed on the task. In his journal, John Leland describes 'a great dok for shippes, and yn this dok lyith yet part of the rybbes of the Henry Grace of Dieu, one of the biggest shippes that hath beene made in homenium memoria [human memory].'[2]

Some two hundred 'men of the country' were needed to man the capstans to wind ships into dock. From 1538, a skill shortage combined with the problems of relying on casual labour resulted in the payment of annuities to some shipwrights, the seeds of a permanent dockyard workforce.

Under Henry VIII, Portsmouth's importance as a dockyard was gradually eclipsed by the old yard at Deptford and the recently established Woolwich yard. Transport costs for conveying shipbuilding materials to the river yards were much cheaper, and they were easier to defend in the event of an attack. Portsmouth declined, and in 1623 the dry dock was filled in, an event that has been described as the 'nadir of (Portsmouth's) career as a naval port'.

During the Dutch wars, which were largely fought in the North Sea, Chatham became the most important yard, but in 1690 King William III ordered that resources be redirected towards the south coast, with a major expansion of Portsmouth and the construction of a new dockyard at Plymouth. A new dry dock and two wet docks were constructed of stone by Edward Dummer, Surveyor of the Naval Board, on land that had been reclaimed from the Harbour. Larger warships were built and fitted out with equipment and materials, requiring more storehouses and workshops. As part of Sir Bernard de Gomme's transformation of the

86 *(top)* View of Dockyard from Old Portsmouth, *c.*1875.

87 *(above)*
Dockyardmen at work, 1875.

88 *(right)*
Launch of torpedo boat carrier *Vulcan* in 1889.

fortifications of Portsmouth, the enlarged Dockyard was surrounded by an earthen rampart topped by a wooden palisade, though this was replaced by a boundary wall and new main entrance made of brick in 1711. Martin-Leake mentions this in his brief description of the Dockyard in the late 1720s, along with officers' houses (now known as Long Row), a dock regiment and a chapel (built in 1704 on the site of what is now Admiralty House). Richard Pococke provides more detail in his account of 1754:

> Most of the Docks are lined with Portland stone and are staunch'd with clay brought from Estamsay (Stamshaw) near. They have from 1,000 to 1,500 men employed in the yard; it is curious to see them go out at the toll of a bell at noon and night, when every one may take out any useless pieces of wood and chips, as much as they can carry under the arm, and small chips in bags, which are examined with a wooden crow, and all of them observed to see that they do not take out any iron, or anything valuable. It is curious to see the forges where they make the anchors; the largest weigh about 80 hundredweight, that is four tons, which are work'd with machines to move them. The ropeyard is 102 fathoms in length ...[3]

In the 1770s, a brick Double Ropehouse, some 1,030 ft. in length, was built as part of a great reorganisation and expansion that took place after the Seven Years War. During this reconstruction the Dockyard continued to work at full capacity, despite an almost continuous 40-year period of naval warfare. New slips were added, dry docks enlarged and more land reclaimed to the north of the yard. By 1800, 20 per cent of the male population of the borough worked in the yard.

Following the appointment of Samuel Bentham as Inspector of Naval Works in 1795, a number of revolutionary developments were pioneered, including the introduction of the first caisson gate (in the Great (No. 1) Basin). The caisson could be filled with water and sunk in the dock entrance to form a seal. When no longer needed, it was emptied, refloated and moved.

The first steam engine, introduced in 1797, was used to pump out the docks' reservoir, an activity previously carried out by two teams of six horses working two capstans. This engine was also used to power a wood saw. Most famously, the factory production of pulley blocks – vital gear for the operation and movement of sails and guns – was initiated under Bentham using machinery developed by Marc Isambard Brunel (father of Isambard Kingdom Brunel). The Block Mills were constructed between 1802-6 and fitted out with the first powered machine tools used for mass production. Blocks, which had previously been hand-made, were now uniformly reliable and one man was able to equal the output of ten skilled blockmakers.

In 1817, Lake Allen described the Dockyard as appearing like a town while functioning as 'undoubtedly the largest naval arsenal in the world'.[4] At the time of his visit there were five ships under construction, though he comments on the dramatic fall in men employed there after the end of the Napoleonic wars.

With peace came no further expansion until the 1840s, prompted by the development of steam vessels that needed longer docks and building slips. Some idea of the impact of steam on working practices in the Yard is given by a visitor in the 1850s:

> In the Factory, the Smitheries and other workshops, it is curious to see the power of steam applied at the same time to the most trifling as well as the most important operations. In one place we see it directed to the cutting of wedges, screws, & c.; in others, drilling, planing, punching and forging. A large fan is driven by it, and air drains made under the floors of the smitheries, convey the blasts to the fires, and thereby supersede the use of bellows. In forging anchors and other heavy iron articles, Nasmith's Patent Steam Hammer is now used.[5]

89 *(left)*
Mobilisation of the Fleet at the
Dockyard, 1904. In the distance can
be seen the tidal basin (left) and
coaling point (right). North Lock (left)
became Lock B in 1912.

90 *(above)*
View of South Lock, looking west,
1904.

While the steam hammer did the work of an
army of blacksmiths, the switch from sail to
steam inevitably closed the Ropery, which had
supplied cordage for hundreds of warships, re-
sulting in 1,500 men being discharged.

The last timber-hulled ship to be built at
Portsmouth was the *Royal Alfred* in 1859. The
first ironclad battleships, such as HMS *Warrior*,
required larger facilities and specialised skills,
and there were fears that the private shipbuilding industry might take over the building and
maintenance of the nation's ships in its defence
against the (perceived) renewed threat from
France. The Admiralty proved that the work
could be carried out just as cost effectively by
the Royal Yards and, in 1864, commissioned the
Great Extension, an ambitious plan to construct
four basins, three docks and two locks.[6] The area
of the Dockyard was more than doubled with
the reclamation of 93 acres of mudflats and the
enclosure of a similar area of Portsea.

The increases in size of warships resulted in
the doubling of tonnage of ships launched
between the 1880s and the 1890s. In 1905 the
most advanced warship in the world, HMS

91 *(above)*
Views of the stern and bow of HMS
Dreadnought taken during its trials
in October 1906.

Dreadnought, was completed in record time. From then until the First World War, one battleship was launched every year in the race for naval supremacy with Germany.

Dreadnought was the first battleship to be powered by steam turbines. Electricity was used for many functions including pumps, fans, hoists and capstans. She was able to fire eight 50 ft. long, 12-inch guns on a broadside with an effective range of 12 miles. *Dreadnought* rendered the rest of the fleet, and most of the docks, obsolete. Two further locks 850 ft. long and 110 ft. wide were built and other docks were adapted and enlarged to cope with this new class of battleship.

The launch of the *Royal Sovereign* in 1915 marked the zenith of shipbuilding at Portsmouth, being the largest and last battleship to be built at the Yard. During the war the workforce doubled to approximately 23,000 (including 1,750 women). Five large submarines were built and 1,200 vessels refitted. The fitting of countermeasures to detect or minimise damage caused by torpedoes, mines and submarines was urgently undertaken, including the installation of bulge protection (against torpedoes) and paravanes (against mines).

The post-war slump hit the Dockyard badly and, by the mid-1920s, the workforce had been reduced to 8,000. Several cruisers were built during this lean

92 *(above)*
This floating dock, the largest in the world at the time, was capable of lifting a dreadnought. It was in use in Fountain Lake between 1912 and 1939.

93 *(right)*
Launch of cruiser HMS *Effingham*, 1921.

94 *(below)*
Launch of dreadnought HMS *Neptune*, 1909.

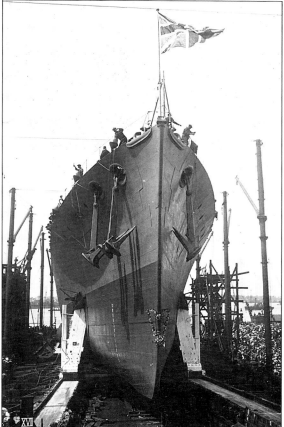

98 *(above)*
Dockyardmen laying the keel plate of
cruiser HMS *London*, 1927.

95 *(top left)*
Dockyard Main Gate showing police
guard and entrance to the Police
Cells on the right, *c.*1901.

96 *(far left)*
A dock being enlarged, *c.*1901.

97 *(left)*
Completion of searchlights for
warships in the Electric Fitting Shop,
*c.*1901.

time, though employment picked up with a modest rearmament programme ten
years later.

By the time the Second World War was declared, the workforce numbered
14,000 men, and 132 women, though this increased to 25,000 at the height of the
war. Some skilled men were recalled after having joined up to fight. Many were
employed installing anti-aircraft guns on merchant ships and trawlers and in the
rapid construction of large numbers of motor minesweepers. Newly developed
devices were installed in warships and other vessels, including radar and counter
measures against acoustic mines and homing torpedoes.[7] The Yard also played a
leading role in the preparation of assault craft for the D-Day landings.

After the war, ship work was generally restricted to refits, repairs, conversions and modernisation. The last ship to be built at Portsmouth in the 20th century was HMS *Andromeda*, launched in 1967. In 1970 the Dockyard Technical College was closed, ending a tradition started in 1843 when the Admiralty established the Royal Dockyard Schools providing apprentices of all trades with daytime and evening classes to supplement their on-the-job training. The courses were seen as a model for engineering education.

In 1981 the Conservative government announced the rundown of the dockyard, and the closure of Chatham as part of the Defence Review, though the Falklands War in 1982 put a temporary stop to thousands of redundancies. Men worked round the clock to prepare the task force and convert merchant vessels for

99 *(above left)*
The Dockyard Iron Foundry, *c.*1904.

100 *(below left)*
Admiral Superintendent and Officers' Residences, The Parade (Long Row), *c.*1904.

101 *(above)*
Men at work finishing the fore barbette of HMS *King Edward VII*, *c.*1904.

102 *(right)*
Battleship in dry dock, *c.*1904.

103
Women at work in the Electrical
Shop, *c*.1916.

104 *(right)*
Pitch House Jetty in 1929. The Dockyard jetties were scenes of many tearful farewells and joyous reunions.

105 *(above)*
South Railway Jetty or 'Farewell Jetty', 1927. A viaduct link to the Harbour Station was opened in 1878 and was used primarily to transport troops and their equipment directly to their troopships. This function was transferred to Southampton in 1894, but the line continued to be used for royal arrivals and departures.

106 *(left)*
The Duke and Duchess of York embark on a tour of the Empire in 1901, on the *Ophir*.

supporting roles. In 1984 the Fleet Maintenance and Repair Organisation (FMRO) took over the duties of the old Royal Dockyard precipitating massive redundancies, and further reorganisation continued this trend. In 2000, Vosper Thorneycroft announced plans to close its Woolston yard and establish the world's most modern warship building facility at Portsmouth, though at the time of writing this was unconfirmed.[8]

Chapter 5

VICTUALLING

107
Jonas Hanway, Commissioner of
Portsmouth Victualling Office, 1762-
83, and founder of the Marine Society
which aided naval recruitment
during the Napoleonic Wars.

Serious consideration appears first to have been given to the organisation and resources necessary to supply ships' crews at the beginning of the 16th century. During the wars with France, Henry VIII ordered the building of a number of breweries and bakeries to serve his expanding navy, but the unreliability of the supply of victuals was well known. The Earl of Surrey had written to the King from the *Mary Rose* anxious 'to do some displeasure to the enemy' but could only do so 'if the wind and victual serve'. He 'doubted much more the victual than the wind'.[1]

The seaman's daily ration, which was established at this time and continued into the 18th century, comprised 1lb. of bread and eight pints of beer, together with varying quantities of meat, butter, cheese, peas and oatmeal. A Royal Brewhouse had been in existence in Portsmouth since 1492, but a further four were built to slake the naval thirst. *The Anchor* bakery and brewhouse on the corner of St Thomas's Street and St Mary's Street was extended to increase capacity, and another bakery, *The Swan*, was built on piles near the Camber. By around 1514 the King's Storehouse had been built to store the navy's beer.[2] By the time of Queen Elizabeth's reign a 'Queene's Greate and Little Cooperadge' was established in King Street, which was later to become part of the Victualling Office.

King's Mill was situated at the head of the Mill Pond and was driven by tidal water passing through a sluice. It was rebuilt on a larger scale in 1744-5 on piles, and was intended to serve the garrison in the event of a siege. By this time flour was supplied to the Victualling Office where six ovens worked non-stop to supply the navy with ship's biscuit, a substitute for bread which was baked two or more times to help preserve it for long voyages. King George II visited the bakery in 1774 and, as he was leaving, ate a fresh one to test its quality, setting a fashion for eating biscuits in the street. But by the time the biscuits reached the men of the Georgian navy, they had often been infected with weevils and mould, due to unsuitable storage. By the 1800s, 65,000 lb. of this 'hard tack' were baked here every week.

During wartime the number of men at sea increased dramatically and there was an increased demand for victuals. Manpower rose from 15,230 in 1775 to

108
Garrison Bakery in King Street,
Portsmouth.

107,446 by the end of the American War of Independence in 1783, a figure that was to be surpassed during the Napoleonic Wars. Stores and other buildings concerned with victualling were built or expanded to meet the demands. In 1776 a slaughter house was erected in St. Mary's Street, where pigs and cattle began their conversion into salt pork and beef, the food that 'was the stuff that gave the fighting stomach to our old seamen'.

Master butchers cut the flesh into 8lb. pieces that were rubbed with salt and saltpetre and preserved in casks topped up with viscous brine. Salted tongues were a delicacy that were rationed according to rank. A victualling agent in Portsmouth in 1705 was instructed to allow seven dozen tongues a year for an admiral, but only one dozen for the lowest seaman.

By 1779 a powder magazine had been built at Priddy's Hard, leaving space in the Square Tower to serve as a meat store. A small pier was built out from the tower, which became known as the Beef Stage.

Corruption was rife in the Victualling Office and prompted inhabitants to petition Parliament. Official investigations discovered widespread abuse in 1783, with systematic fraud, equipment and supplies being routinely stolen and sold on, and certain contractors being favoured. A disproportionate number of victualling contracts in the first half of the 18th century do appear to have been awarded to contractors who were Portsmouth aldermen.

The Commissioner of the Victualling Office at the time of the investigations was the philanthropist Jonas Hanway, whose headquarters were on top of the Square Tower. Hanway developed pioneering ideas on diet and health and published a thesis on the advantages of wholemeal bread in 1773. He advocated beer drinking for working men, arguing that it was 'an essential article to his health, as well as the joy to his heart'. Less popular was his recommendation that people should wash at least once a week. Hanway was also famous for having popularised

the umbrella in this country, and for having co-founded the Marine Society which trained poor young vagrants for naval service.

Local contractors thrived during the Napoleonic Wars. In 1802, Portsmouth baker Edward Tollervey bought Lumley watermill at Emsworth and established the hub of a business empire. The flour produced by his mills was used to produce ships' biscuit, while waste was used to fatten up livestock which was also destined for the sailor's plate.

By 1827 the dispersed victualling offices and storehouses in Portsmouth were in need of extensive repairs, and the decision was made to save money and bring all the functions together on one site. The Brewery and Cooperage at Weevil Yard in Gosport already supplied beer, wine and water to the Navy, drawing on a 360 ft. deep artesian well. The creek had been deepened and wharves constructed in the 1750s. A steam mill, bakehouse, kiln, slaughterhouse, offices and storehouses were constructed and further mud banks cleared in preparation for its new function. The Portsmouth premises were sold off in 1832, and the Royal Clarence Yard established. It was named in 1831 after the Duke of Clarence who had decreed that it should be developed as a fully fledged victualling yard.

The storekeeper at this time was Thomas Tassell Grant, a native of Portsea who came up with a number of inventions to improve the quality and conditions for men at sea. The reputation of Clarence Yard as a biscuit-maker has been attributed to Grant, whose steam-powered biscuit-making machinery was capable of baking 10,000 biscuits in an hour. Previously, ship-biscuit was a labour-intensive occupation involving a driver, who mixed the ingredients in a giant trough, a breakman, who kneaded the dough on a platform called a break, and an idleman, mate and furner who helped cut and mould and bake the dough. Before being baked, the biscuits were pierced with holes with an instrument called a docker. The nine ovens in the Clarence bakehouse employed 45 men and the cost of production per hundredweight was 19d., compared with 5¼d. using mechanised production.[3]

In 1838, nearly eleven million pounds of biscuit were produced at the yard, reflecting its importance in the sailor's diet. An anonymous lady visitor to the Yard in 1854 watched the new technology with a sense of wonder. After revolving cylinders winnowed and cleaned the wheat, thirty millstones ground it, cylindrical sieves separated the bran and a conveyor belt of dozens of buckets carried it to be mechanically turned into dough:

> We then went into a long room swarming with pale-faced bakers. Steam
> here mixes the dough, rolls it flat, cuts it into squares, stamps it, and
> when the men have put it into the ovens, steam carries it back the trays
> to the other end of the room.[4]

At the time of this visit, production was continuing night and day to supply the Baltic Fleet in preparation for the Crimean War. As well as providing fuel for the fighting men of the navy, 'Gosport biscuits' are said to have prevented famine after the Siege of Paris in 1871, when a fleet of freight ships ran from Gosport to Le Havre. Trials of baking bread on ships had taken place in the 1860s, but it was not until the 1900s that electric ovens began to provide sailors with fresh bread at sea, leading to the end of biscuit making at Clarence in 1907.

Grant also invented a distillation machine to convert sea water into drinking water, which was used during the Crimean War. He was promoted to Controller of

110
Offices of the Victualling Store Department, Royal Clarence Yard, *c*.1901.

Victualling and Transport Services and his responsibilities came to include the provision of clothing, utensils and other equipment to the Navy, as well as large quantities of bedding for troops on passage to India and other Imperial service.

The discovery that meat could be preserved by canning led to the gradual decline of salted meat. Most foodstuffs and equipment arrived and left by water until the railway was built in the 1840s. Despite the emphasis on quality control, private contractors hired to supply provisions tended to put their profits above the comforts of fighting men. Canned beef which had been bought in was found to consist of putrid offal, and consignments of warm clothing and boots intended for soldiers to cope with the Russian winters during the Crimean War turned out to be all left-footed or otherwise hopelessly inadequate.

Cattle arrived either 'on the hoof' from local contractors, or were imported by ship and landed in the yard by steam crane, and were herded into pens where they were examined for signs of disease before slaughter. Meat was supplied to the fleet after having been salted and barrelled, but was also used to feed Marines at Forton, staff and patients at Haslar Hospital and boys on the training ships. The livestock was taken from the Lairs to the slaughter house, which was situated in the northeast corner of the yard, directly opposite Burrow Island. This small island in Portsmouth Harbour is said to have acquired the name Rat Island in the 19th century because rats gathered there to gorge themselves on discarded entrails from the abattoir.

111
A 'Gosport biscuit'.

112
Coopers at Clarence Yard making casks for salt beef, c.1901.

113 *(top)*
Royal Clarence Yard Main Gate,
*c.*1920.

114 *(left)*
The Abattoir at Royal Clarence Yard,
*c.*1901.

115 *(below left)*
Hoisting in flour, *c.*1925.

116 *(below)*
Distribution of rum rations on
Christmas Day, *c.*1925.

117 *(right)*
Bakery on board HMS *Triumph,*
*c.*1914.

Apart from the brewing of beer, rum was also blended and barrelled at the Yard. This gradually superseded beer as a ration item, and was watered down aboard ship and served as grog. The cooperage remained in use until the abolition of the naval rum issue in 1970.

The Royal Clarence Yard, together with the Victoria Yard at Deptford and the William Yard at Stonehouse, may be said to have been the first large-scale food-processing factories in the country. Clarence Yard experienced the most extreme test of its capacity and organisation to provide and distribute provisions during the Second World War, when it became clear that there was insufficient space to store the provisions demanded by the fleet. Additional storage areas were found in local buildings, including the Bus Depot at Hoeford. The problem was made worse following the bombing raids of early 1941 when the Meat Store, Cooperage Shed and Clothing Stores were destroyed. Many of the Yard's functions were dispersed to safer areas of southern England as work began in 1942 for the vital supply of provisions to the D-Day forces as they prepared to liberate Europe. By April 1944, the assembled fleet at Spithead was being supplied with 140,000 tons of fresh water, a quarter of a million lb. of bread, a million lb. of potatoes and a quarter million lb. of meat every week. A further million packages of other provisions were distributed during the months of May and June, a massive round-the-clock operation

which involved men from the New Barracks and a large female work force. Any available person with experience of boats was requisitioned to deliver the supplies. Following the war, demand inevitably declined and the grunts of livestock and the tapping of coopers gave way to the whine of fork-lift trucks and the hum of deep refrigeration. In 1991 the clothing stocks were moved to Portsmouth, leaving only a Store Depot which, with the contracting out of NAAFI functions, became redundant. After nearly 170 years of victualling the fleet, Royal Clarence Yard was finally closed in April 1995.[5]

The nearby Forton Fuel Depot, however, continued its role of storing and supplying the Navy's fuel. The *Queen Elizabeth*, built at Portsmouth Dockyard and launched in 1913, was the first battleship to use oil as its sole fuel, making it cleaner and easier to supply than coal. Most battleships in the First World War, however, used coal, which was supplied from coaling vessels. The scene in Portsmouth Harbour in 1910 is described by the *Illustrated London News*:

> Towering black hulls, laden with coal, swing their forest of Temperley transporters over the greedy hatches alongside, and in the far distance,

118 *(above)*
Temperley transporters coaling a ship, c.1904.

119 *(above right)*
The largest coaling vessel in the world, *C1*, under construction in 1904.

120 *(right)*
Aerial view of Portsmouth Harbour in 1914, showing *C1* off Burrow Island.

against the background of Portsdown Hill, can be seen the slender yellow funnels and masts of the Royal Yachts.[6]

The most prominent coaling vessel, the largest in the world and rather less elegant than a Royal Yacht, was known as *C1*. Built by Swan Hunter and brought to Portsmouth in 1904, it dominated the harbour scene for sixty years. Moored in the harbour off Rat Island, *C1* was longer than a football pitch and could hold 12,000 tons of coal, which was supplied to the vessel by colliers. Coal was loaded

into ships' holds using an electrically operated Temperley transporter which consisted of a system of trolleys by which huge, suspended buckets moved along an outstretched boom. In 1925, *C1* was moved to a position off Hardway and used the following year during the General Strike as a depot for imported coal. In the Second World War she coaled many of the ships used in the evacuation of over 200,000 British troops from Dunkirk. But the gradual phasing out of coal as a marine fuel eventually led to redundancy, and in 1964 she left the harbour for the breakers' yard.

Apart from ease of supply, oil also had the advantage over coal in that no black smoke was created to give a ship's position away. Forton Fuel Depot was in use by the time of the First World War, when a Dockyard employee was arrested for spying there.[7] The risk posed by air raids in the Second World War led to the relocation of the depot to a site west of Fort Southwick where large underground fuel tanks were installed. By the 1990s, Fuel and Armament Depots and Victualling organisations were controlled by the Royal Naval Supply and Transport Service.

121
Men at work in the Central Passage of *C1*, *c.*1905.

122
Stokers feeding the furnaces of a warship, *c.*1916.

Chapter 6

FEEDING THE GUNS

123
The Square Tower in 1729, when it served as a powder magazine, showing its close proximity to dwelling houses.

In 1526, Cornelys Johnson, Henry VIII's Master Smith for Ordnance in Portsmouth, compiled an inventory describing the bad state of guns in the port. Johnson counted 397 iron and brass serpentines (or matchlocks) in states of disrepair.[1] Even when working properly, a drop of rain or a gust of wind rendered this weapon useless, and French bowman are said to have laughed at them.

Henry VIII was an enthusiast for the cannon and encouraged its manufacture and development in England, having been upset that the best cannon had to be imported. Some of the earliest examples of artillery appear to have been used in defence of the port, including wooden cannon with barrels strengthened by iron hoops. An example was recovered off Spithead, near the wreck of the *Mary Rose*. Often the men manning this type of breech-loading cannon were killed when it was fired, but during Henry's reign the muzzle loader was introduced and proved far safer and more effective.

The Dissolution of the Monasteries brought the conversion of the Domus Dei (later the Royal Garrison Church) into an armoury. An inventory from 1547 lists 'shott of yrone … morispickes, chestes of bowes and arrowes, serpentyne powder … cassemements with hand gonnes and bowstrings (and other) munychions …'.

The building of the Square Tower was started in 1494, and was originally designed to carry artillery, but from the end of the 16th century until around 1779, it served as a powder magazine, with a capacity of up to 12,000 barrels of gunpowder. Its presence at the end of the High Street so close to dwelling houses and taverns caused great concern among the population, who submitted a petition to the Master General of Ordnance in 1716. They argued that it would be an ideal target for bombardment in the event of an enemy attack from the sea. There was also concern that smoking, drunken sailors gathered dangerously close to the gunpowder when it was being transported, and that often the barrels leaked leaving a fuse trail along the street. Following an explosion that caused extensive damage, another petition was made in 1767 and the Ordnance Board conceded. A remote area of land in Gosport had been bought with a view to extending the Gosport fortifications, but was now given over to the building of a powder magazine, storehouses and cooperage. By 1777, ships in the Harbour were being supplied with armaments from Priddy's Hard, named after one of the former landowners, Jane Priddy.

The powder magazine was solidly built with massive buttresses. No iron was used in its construction to minimise the risk of sparks igniting the 400,000 lb. of gunpowder that was stored there. During the conflict with France, it was found that additional storage space was needed for the vast quantities of gunpowder needed by the fleet. A Royal Powder Works appears to have been in use on Little Horsea in the 18th century, and a large bomb-proof magazine was constructed at Tipner Point in around 1800 with room for 24,000 barrels.

From 1801 to 1918, a total of 12 obsolete wooden warships were also used as floating magazines or 'powder hulks' in Portsmouth Harbour. This practice was favoured by the Admiralty because of the reduced risk to nearby property in the

124
Gunwharf Gate, *c*.1899.

event of an explosion, and the availability of gunpowder and guncotton at very short notice to supply the fleet. These storage depots and hulks complemented the work at the Gunwharf, which supplied and maintained guns, small arms and other ordnance.

What became known as the Gunwharf comprised two separate gunwharves which projected into Portsmouth Harbour on either side of a creek that led to the Mill Pond, on the site of what is now the United Services Ground. Building of the Old Gunwharf, on the Dockyard side of the creek, began in 1662, with the reclamation of an area of some 60,000 square yards, a massive excavation involving the removal of soil from areas to the south of Queen Street. The huge army of workers were paid in a pub in Bishop Street named *The Shakespeare's Head* after the contractor, a William Shakespeare. Thick stone walls were built to contain the soil, with the wharf projecting 350 yards into the Harbour. A Clerk in the Navy Pay Office, Stephen Martin-Leake, wrote in 1729 that 'the Ordnance is a pretty neat place; it runs west into the harbour, just beyond the Mill Gate, flanking the covert way. Here they have a line of guns upon land carriages, which they fire upon rejoicing days, and hoist the Union flag upon a tall flagstaff.'[2]

The start of the Napoleonic Wars in 1793 prompted a review of both the Gunwharf and the Dockyard. By 1797 the storehouses, armouries and Royal Artillery barracks had proved inadequate and a second New Gunwharf on the Camber side was commissioned by the Board of Ordnance. Soil was used from the excavation of the new South Dock in the Dockyard and the work was completed in 1814. The two Gunwharves were linked by a bridge.

The foundation stone for the Grand Storehouse was laid by the Duke of Clarence in 1811. Dr. Henry Slight, writing in the 1820s, was impressed: 'This magnificent building, which is of red brick and stone, presents a massive front towards the town, and three sides of a square towards the sea, having in its centre a noble archway, surmounted by a lofty tower and cupola, containing an excellent clock. It contains the battering-train, gun carriages, and every description of ordnance store ready at a moment's notice.'[3] It was used temporarily as part of the Mining School during the First World War, and renamed the Vulcan Building. Between the wars, as part of HMS *Vernon*, it housed torpedo and mine design departments, but was badly damaged by incendiaries in 1941.

Visitors to the Gunwharves in the 19th century were astonished by the scale of arms and munitions kept at the Grand Storehouse, with hundreds of huge mortars and cannon neatly arranged in parallel rows and pyramids of up to 40,000 cannonballs and shells. Cannon ranged from 3 pounders to guns of 30 tons, including new ones for ships yet to be built and those belonging to ships in dock. The stores and magazines contained 21,000 rifles, other small arms, boarding hooks and gun carriages.[4]

The Board of Ordnance, which had been responsible for all guns and ammunition used by both the Navy and Army, was accused of inefficiency and abolished in 1855 despite protestations that it was being used as a scapegoat for mismanagement during the Crimean War. In 1888 a stocktaking review split the Gunwharves, with the Old Gunwharf given over to military ordnance and the Navy allocated the New Gunwharf. Small arms and early machine guns were stored in the former Royal Artillery barracks, while temporary stores were erected to meet the increasing demand of ships attached to the Portsmouth command.

In 1915 the whole of the Gunwharf site was transferred to the Admiralty to cope with the demands of war while the Army Ordnance Corps was based at Hilsea, the Board of Ordnance having bought Gatcombe House and the surrounding land and added it to Hilsea Barracks in the 19th century. Local women were employed in large numbers making munitions and repairing tents and other equipment. In 1921, the barracks were vacated by the Royal Field Artillery and the whole site became the principal Army Ordnance Depot.

125 *(far left)*
Grand Storehouse, Gunwharf, 1855.

126 *(below)*
The old Gunwharf Armoury, *c*.1900.

127 *(bottom)*
Interior of Gunwharf Armoury, *c*.1900.

The original 18th-century buildings at Priddy's Hard included a shifting house, where workers could change their contaminated clothes, a small barracks and a guard house. Increasing demand, together with new developments in explosives technology, led to an expansion in buildings for storage and maintenance, with over thirty new buildings being added between 1861 and 1904. By 1900, over 300 men and boys were engaged in preparing ammunition. They were often searched for matches and keys at the gate, and had to change into special shoes and clothes with bone buttons to prevent friction.[5] Small shell filling rooms were built surrounded by earthworks to limit damage in the event of accidents.

A further 55 buildings were added during the First World War. Three piers enabled shells and other munitions to be loaded and transported to the Fleet. Large numbers of local women were brought in to cope with demand, often on hazardous work like cartridge filling and TNT bagging. One of the perils associated with shell filling was toxic jaundice caused by TNT poisoning, a condition which turned the workers' faces bright yellow and earned them the nickname 'the canaries'.

After the First World War, the naval functions of the Gunwharf were transferred to Priddy's Hard where another New Gunwharf was constructed between 1918 and 1920. In the new factory and workshops highly skilled men carried out repairs on small arms such as Lee-Enfield rifles, while others worked on large calibre guns up to 15 inches, weighing 100 tons.

The Mining School section of HMS *Vernon* moved ashore to the Portsmouth Gunwharf site during the First World War when the importance of the weapon in modern warfare became evident. But limited space made it inappropriate for development into a new Mining Depot, though instructional and experimental functions remained at *Vernon*. An alternative site was sought, and by 1918 Royal Marine Engineers were employed in the construction of a new depot at Frater. Here, mines were examined, tested, serviced and stored, prior to transportation by rail to Bedenham Pier where they were loaded into lighters for transit to mine-laying vessels. By the Second World War, increased staff training was carried out to deal with the complex technology of mine warfare. Magnetic, acoustic and antenna mines were chemically charged at Frater, and limpet, aircraft, and submarine mines were among others handled and supplied from here. In 1959, Frater ceased mine work and was renamed as a Royal Naval Armament Depot, responsible for the repair of torpedoes, guns and anti-submarine weapons. This continued the work previously carried out at the Torpedo Depot in Portsmouth Dockyard, which serviced virtually every type of torpedo used by the Navy from 1884 until its closure in 1959.

Bedenham Magazine Depot was built in the years leading up to the First World War. Its wooden pier was used to land cordite supplies from the Royal Naval Cordite Factory at Horton Heath, Dorset, which began production in 1914. A wharf was also constructed at Frater in 1917 to assist in the supply of shells to the Fleet. In the 1920s another magazine depot was established near Fort Elson. This was converted into a guided missile repair facility in the 1960s.

Manually operated small gauge rail systems were in use at Priddy's from the 1880s, but a broad gauge line was laid during 1912/13, and connected Frater Depot

128 *(above and right)*
First World War workers in the Portsmouth area.

129 *(below)*
First World War munition workers and badge.

130 *(above left)*
Priddy's Hard sign at Hardway entrance.

131 *(above right)*
Loading a 4.7 gun on HM Gunboat *Comet* at Portsmouth.

132 *(left)*
Munition workers at Priddy's Hard in 1944. This group, which includes Elsie Mullins and Lilian Harbut (2nd row, first and second left), was employed on fitting fuses.

with the main rail network via the level crossing near the Main Gate. As a safeguard, 'fireless' locomotives were used on the line, which was gradually extended to connect Bedenham, Frater, Priddy's Hard and Elson.

During the Second World War, staffing at Priddy's Hard trebled to 3,700 from its pre-war level. Altogether 1,700 women workers were involved in the massive build up of arms for D-Day.

In 1977, Priddy's Hard, Frater, Bedenham and Elson were unified under Royal Naval Armaments Depot (RNAD) control, and provided support during the Falklands War. A further reorganisation led to the closure of Priddy's in 1989. The RNAD continued at its other sites with a staff of 850, and was responsible for the maintenance and storage of the complete range of conventional ammunition, pyrotechnics and demolition stores, including plastic explosives. Nuclear depth charges are also said to have been stored at Frater. Guided weapons maintained included Exocet, Seadart and Seacat and the Sting Ray torpedo. Into the new millennium, in common with many other defence establishments, RNAD is working closely with commercial companies to develop new weapon systems, such as the Sea Wolf guided missile.

Chapter 7

Naval Recruitment and Education

133
'A Press-Gang at Work', by
Rowlandson.

The impressment of men for service in the Royal Navy was a right claimed by the
Crown and continued until the early 19th century. In peacetime enough men and
boys from the lower classes could usually be relied upon to join the Navy volun-
tarily to escape from poverty. For growing boys of 12, or even younger, the prospect
of a pound of meat four times a week was a temptation. Few working men could
afford that. But in wartime, the press gangs were sent out at night to gather the
thousands of men needed to fill the fighting ships of the fleet. Legally only merchant seamen and seafaring men like fishermen could be pressed. Thus, in
November 1776, it was reported that 'scarce a fish or even an oyster is to be got'
because of the press gangs' activities in the Portsmouth area. But there was also
widespread impressment of landsmen during national emergencies when the 'hot
press' took place. During one such 'hot press' in Portsmouth throughout March
1803, alehouses were raided, private houses broken into and informers were paid
20 shillings per head.[1] In this climate, Gosport watermen hid at home, stranding
people wanting to cross the harbour. A report from this time describes how men
who were visiting a fair with their girlfriends changed clothes with them when the
press gang arrived. The women, it seems, were pressed and there were 'hilarious
scenes at the rendezvous when the surgeons commenced the medicals'. But, more
serious than mistakes over gender, were those over class. Inevitably 'respectable
townsmen' were sometimes taken by the gangs, but provided they could later
prove their high standing in the town they were released.

Pub landlords adapted their premises to hide their valued customers from the
press gangs. Before converting the *Fountain Inn* in the High Street into the Soldiers' Institute, Sarah Robinson reported finding a secret staircase and hiding
places on every floor behind the dark wood panelling.

The scale of the 'hot press' operation was impressive. In September 1803 about
thirty gangs comprising some 600 men worked Portsmouth at once, picking up
'many useful hands' who were imprisoned in the Guard House on Grand Parade.
On another occasion a Captain Bowen spread rumours of a riot at Fort Monckton,
and as local inhabitants trooped over Haslar Bridge to satisfy their curiosity,

Captain Bowen's party of marines blocked off the bridge and took their pick of the men, raising 500 in a day.

Some gang members were receptive to bribery, if a pressed man had the means. This arrangement appears to have been formalised in the 1800s by the setting up of an agency in Hawke Street, where, for an average fee of ten guineas, a substitute could be found to fill your shoes.

Impressment was not the only means of recruitment used. Pressure was put on local authorities to help persuade men to enlist, and specific quotas were set. Magistrates would sentence those found guilty of crimes such as smuggling to several years of navy service. Bounties were also offered for volunteers to enlist, and this sometimes attracted better educated men who were in debt. These 'quota men' were blamed by some for stirring up discontent among their shipmates by discussing democratic ideas. The mutinies at Spithead and the Nore in 1797 were mainly led by former professional people who had enlisted in this way.

In 1756, before he became Commissioner of the Victualling Office, Jonas Hanway founded the London-based Marine Society. This successfully channelled poor boys, vagrants and criminals into the Navy and arranged that they be clothed and cared for on their return. Hanway is credited with having provided more men for the Navy than any other man in history, with 23,000 having entered the service under the scheme between 1793-1815.[2]

By the end of the Napoleonic Wars, press gangs had ceased to be used. The effect of kidnapping local tradesmen, both in terms of the local economy and on the families left behind, is incalculable, but it was also counter-productive for the Navy. The Admiralty was beginning to recognise the importance of morale on board the ships of the fleet. However, after 1815, it sometimes took several months to fully man a ship once it had been commissioned.

A seaman's normal term of service was only for the commission of the ship, which could vary from a few months to three or four years. With the establishment of the Gunnery School on HMS *Excellent* in Portsmouth Harbour, a new sort of recruit had to be attracted, and part of the enhanced terms of engagement included continuous service. This meant five or seven years at an increased rate of pay, with the option of a further five years. Continuous service was eventually introduced to the Navy to help solve the manning problem.

By the middle of the 19th century, recruitment agents came in a number of guises:

> The Hard is a horrible locality. All the houses that are not taverns with vulgar names, are pawnbrokers and slop shops. The windows of most were full of giant placards, offering unheard-of advantages, even beyond death, to men patriotic enough to serve their country in various ships with the most belligerent names.[3]

134
Recruitment poster, *c.*1931.

135
Naval Recruiting Office at The Hard.

136
The Naval Academy, later renamed the Royal Naval College.

One of the most famous of these recruitment centres on the Hard was the *St Vincent* public house, where the landlady, a Miss Wayford, is reported to have exerted great powers of persuasion over drinkers in her establishment, directing them to specific ships with reassurances about the good times that lay ahead of them.[4] But by the 1880s there were more formal arrangements, with the opening of a Royal Naval Recruiting Office at the Hard (now the Tourist Information Office), which was in operation until the early 1920s.

Before the early years of the 18th century, young naval officers were educated at sea, relying upon the patronage of ships' captains to gain their training. This situation inevitably led to captains choosing from their friends and relations, who were sometimes entered on the ships' books as infants. This resulted in a great variation in standards, and children as young as eight going to war. To overcome this, the Navy Board agreed to provide a limited number of sons of officers and gentlemen, between the ages of 13 and 16, with a comprehensive, formal training. The Naval Academy was built in the south-east corner of the Dockyard in 1733. The academy, the first naval training shore establishment in the country, opened with a curriculum that included navigation, gunnery, fencing, French and dancing. A visitor in 1754 was impressed with the regime:

> The Academy is a handsom building for fifty youths to be instructed in the theory and practice of Navigation, where they are lodged, dieted and wear the sea officers uniform, blue turn'd up with white; here they remain three years and are made midshipmen; and this, or serving under captains of men-of-war three years, is the only way of being advanced in the Navy. They go out once a week and work a yacht, which is full rigg'd as a man-of-war, in order to be well versed in the practice … they have a fine orrery which cost £200, and a model of a first rate man-of-war rig'd …[5]

Though there can be little doubt that the training provided was a great improvement over serving in a man-of-war, the academy was unpopular with the nobility and with captains who had lost much of their influence over who should be trained for the officer class. One of Jane Austen's brothers was a scholar here in the 1790s.

The college does appear to have been poorly managed, with reports of ill-discipline, expulsions and head lice. In 1801, Admiral Lord St Vincent wrote that the college was 'a sink of vice and abomination', reflecting the situation a few yards away in Portsea, on the other side of the Dockyard wall.

In 1806 the academy was renamed the Royal Naval College, and under the firm leadership of the Reverend James Inman, gained respect and credibility. The nearby School of Naval Architecture, intended 'for the education of a superior class of shipwright apprentices', was incorporated into the college in 1816. Inman compiled a standard naval text, *Navigation and Astronomy for the use of British Seamen*, in his residence in the left wing, making use of the distinctive cupola which served as an observatory. The cupola had a gallery from which students manoeuvred models of ships of the fleet on the floor below. Two sergeants of the Royal Marine Artillery gave instruction in the use of cannon.

In 1835 Captain Hastings of HMS *Excellent* became Superintendent, beginning a close association between the two establishments that reflected the importance of mathematics in the training of seaman gunners. In 1874-5, the College moved to Greenwich, and the old building served as quarters for officers studying

137
Training Ship HMS *St Vincent*, *c*.1895.

gunnery, torpedo and pilotage. In 1906 it became the Royal Naval School of Navigation and was named after the gunboat HMS *Dryad*, one of the tenders allocated to the school.

If the nobility or gentry had doubts about the Royal Naval College, Gosport offered a private alternative. In 1791, Dr. William Burney established a school in Clarence Square overlooking the harbour at Gosport, the aims of which were to prepare their sons for naval, military and diplomatic service at a senior level. Both William and his son Henry, who succeeded him, appear to have been very fond of the cane. Famous alumni of Burney's Academy included Admiral Togo, Admiral Beatty and General Sam Browne. The school moved to Surrey in 1904.

138
The training brig *Martin* under sail off Clarence Pier, *c.*1897.

In 1841, another preparatory school for the 'sons of noblemen and gentlemen' was founded by the curate of Crofton, Rev. William Foster, at Stubbington House in Stubbington. William Foster had previously been headmaster of St Paul's Grammar School in Southsea, and had also published books on Latin and Greek grammar and algebra. His new school established a reputation as the ideal place to send future naval entrants, many of who were then passed to the training ship *Britannia* at Dartmouth. The school flourished throughout the 19th-century under William and his descendants. A separate part of the school was used to coach boys for Army examinations and entry into Sandhurst and Woolwich, but it was as 'the cradle of the Navy' that the school became famous, providing up to a third of all new entrants to the service. Old boys included Captain Robert Falcon Scott of the Antarctic, Lord Charles Beresford, the Admirals Cunningham and latterly Sir John Woodward. The school survived at Stubbington until 1962, when it moved to Earlywood near Ascot.

Another private school for boys waiting to enter the Royal Navy as cadets was founded in Portsmouth by Thomas Eastman, an ex-Naval Instructor of HMS *Excellent*. It opened in St George's Square, Portsea in 1851, but moved to 28 Eastern Parade (now South Parade) in 1854. Eastman's Royal Naval Academy, or ERNA, as it was known, counted Admiral Sir Percy Scott and Field Marshal John French amongst its famous alumni. From 1911, it was known as Eastman's Preparatory School until its closure in the Second World War.

The first formal officer training on training ships, as opposed to the occasional hands-on training available at the old Royal Naval College, was established in 1857 on the old wooden *Illustrious*, which was moored in Portsmouth Harbour. Under the command of Captain Robert Harris, recruits were trained in navigation and drill and practical aspects of seamanship on the 311-ton brig *Sealark*.

Training of ordinary seamen had taken place under Captain Harris on the *Illustrious* since 1854. Known as 'Jemmy Graham's novices', after the First Lord, the seamen boys acquired a good reputation, but it appears that the training of all social classes on the same ship was not considered either practical or desirable and so the *Illustrious* was devoted solely to officer training. Within seven years the larger *Britannia* replaced the *Illustrious*, and it was decided to remove initial officer training from Portsmouth completely. *Britannia* was moved to Dartmouth in 1863, later to be replaced by a new Naval College which was built at Dartmouth in 1905. Officers spent two years at another new training establishment, Osborne College on the Isle of Wight, before completing their training at Dartmouth.

In 1863 the *St Vincent* was converted into a training ship for seamen boys, the old wooden ship becoming a familiar part of the harbour seascape for over forty years. Recruits were provided with lodgings at a hostel in South Street, Gosport. After nine months on board *St Vincent*, boys were sent out in training brigs in crews of 100 to learn sail drill, steering and signalling. The emphasis was on character building, discipline and instilling a sense of individual responsibility for the ship. The sail and spar drill high above deck was 'of invaluable moral effect for hardening the nerve', though the practical relevance of such training was questioned by some. By 1903, this drill had been abolished and the old brigs were replaced by steam vessels. On completion of their training boys were drafted to a modern battleship or cruiser, providing a stark contrast to the working conditions aboard *St Vincent*.

In 1905, training at *St Vincent* was transferred to a shore establishment at Shotley, but in 1927, it was recommissioned as a shore establishment at Forton Barracks which had been vacated three years earlier by the Royal Marine Light Infantry. A 110ft. mast was erected to continue the tradition of testing boys' nerves and skill. Training was interrupted only by the temporary transfer of the base to the Fleet Air Arm and to *Vernon*'s torpedo trainers during the Second World War.

A reorganisation of naval training carried out in 1968 signalled the end of the 'nursery of the Navy' when its functions were transferred to HMS *Raleigh* at Torpoint.[6] A secondary school was built on the site which later became a sixth form college.

139 *(top)*
Furling and stowing the head sails, *St Vincent*, c.1903.

140 *(above)*
Splicing a hemp rope, c.1897.

141 *(top)*
St Vincent boys' display team performing on the New (St George) Barracks field in the 1930s.

142 *(above)*
St Vincent boathouse in the 1930s. (Mill Lane is on the left.)

143 *(above right)*
Training in the use of anchors at *St Vincent* in the 1930s.

Less formal training was offered from 1932 until the outbreak of war on the 'wooden walls', *Implacable* and *Foudroyant*, in Portsmouth Harbour. The Society for Nautical Research, anxious to preserve the ships and keep the old traditions alive, advertised 'vacational training in seamanship', emphasising the advantages of having someone else look after your children during the holiday, while instilling discipline. The frigate *Foudroyant* continued the holidays for up to 100 boys and girls in 1950, under the supervision of Lt. Col. Harold Wyllie.[7]

While sail training was kept alive for nostalgic and character-building qualities, the real business of training young men to run and maintain modern warships continued, albeit in old, rotting hulks. During the 1880s, the three-decked *Marlborough* served as a college for seamen engineers while moored in the

Dockyard. By 1906, the Portsmouth Harbour-based HMS *Fisgard* was one of three establishments chosen to carry out a training scheme for the creation of Engine Room Artificers, the others being at Chatham and Devonport. Admiral Jacky Fisher introduced the scheme because he did not trust boys trained outside the Navy, believing them to be tainted by trade unions. After the First World War, the three establishments were combined at *Fisgard*, which by now comprised four old warships shackled together at the end of a long rickety wooden pier at Hardway, including the *Spartiate* (*Fisgard* I), *Calcutta* (*Fisgard* II) and *Terrible* (*Fisgard* III). From 700 to 1,200 Artificer Apprentices, or 'tiffy boys', between the ages of 15 and 20, were in training at any one time at the Naval Mechanical Training Establishment, their spartan living quarters being on the former HMS *Terrible*, while the workshops were contained within the former *Hindustan* and *Sultan*. They learned all the practical skills necessary for the maintenance and running of most of the machinery in a warship, along with the underlying theories of marine engineering and advanced mathematics. Boys specialised in a particular trade, qualifying as a coppersmith, boiler maker, engine smith or fitter and turner at the end of their training. The cramped living conditions made sport an important part of the regime, with rugby and 20-mile cross-country runs every week, led by a 'muscular Christian' padre, on the fields at Hardway and around Gosport. The legendary cricketer C.B. Fry brought a team of boys every year to play at Hardway from the training ship *Mercury* which he ran on the Hamble.

The old ships had deteriorated badly in the few years they were at Hardway and, by 1932, could no longer be used. The last batch of apprentices were transferred to Chatham and the *Spartiate*, *Calcutta* and *Terrible* were broken up, while the *Sultan* was transferred to the Dockyard and adapted to train stokers. *Fisgard*'s brief but fondly remembered association with the Portsmouth area was over.

Training in other, more specialised, branches of the Navy such as gunnery, torpedo and navigation are dealt with in the following chapters.

144 *(top)*
Foudroyant at Portsmouth.

145 *(bottom)*
'Tiffy boys' in the Fitting Shop, *Fisgard*.

Chapter 8

NAVAL GUNNERY TRAINING

146
Small arms training, 1896.

In the late 1820s there was a growing recognition among some high-ranking naval officers that the service was manned by 'damned fine seamen but damned bad gunners'. By 1830 the Board of Admiralty had been persuaded to take steps to address the problem, and HMS *Excellent* was established as a School of Gunnery. The wooden ship was moored off the north-west corner of the Dockyard, her port broadside facing towards Fareham Creek. Under the instruction of a Marine Artillery detachment, seamen were trained to fire and maintain every type of gun used in the Fleet, with targets and range markers being set up on the mud flats. A theory of gunnery was taught, together with a solid grounding in mathematics, an education that was appreciated by the trainees, many of who lacked any formal education. The foundations of the Navy's Range Tables were laid here under *Excellent*'s first Commander, George Smith. In 1839, close ties were forged with the Royal Naval Academy in the Dockyard when Smith's successor, Captain Hastings, was made Superintendent. The effectiveness of the newly trained naval gunners was established at the Battle of Acre in 1840, when a formidable Egyptian fortress was bombarded and captured.

The ship *Excellent* was broken up in 1834 and the *Boyne* fitted out as the Gunnery School, which, in turn, was replaced by the *Charlotte* in 1859, both having been renamed *Excellent* during their service.

In the early 1850s, two dry mudbanks in Portsmouth Harbour called Waley, together with Burrow Island, were appropriated for rifle drill and field training and, in 1864, a small brick building was erected on Waley. Thousands of tons of spoil, excavated from successive new Dockyard basins, were dumped on the mudbanks by an army of convict labourers. The waste was transported by rail along a pile viaduct to the site which gradually expanded to form an island of 70 acres. Lieutenant Percy Scott, who joined *Excellent* to qualify as a Gunnery Lieutenant in 1878, suggested that the island be levelled and drained and that the school transfer there, an idea that shocked brine-blooded, sail drill die-hards. Seven years later, with the support of Captain Jacky Fisher, the plan won Admiralty approval and, by

1890, the renamed Whale Island was habitable. Percy Scott served as Commander while the new Gunnery School took shape. Barracks, classrooms, an armourer's shop, a magazine and drill shed, canteens, washrooms, clothing stores and a sick bay were erected to form what soon became the largest gunnery school in the world. Sports and leisure facilities included reading rooms, a gymnasium, tennis courts, cricket and football pitches, a bowling alley, and a set of clay pigeon traps. In 1896 a pigeon house was built and *Excellent* became the Royal Navy's nursery of homing pigeons.

A floating bridge to the mainland worked by wire and winch was operational by 1891, and was able to transfer 100 fully equipped men every trip. This service was unofficially augmented by local boatmen who charged a half-penny a head to ferry sailors from Stamshaw to Whale Island, though this toll doubled for a night crossing. At low-tide the short distance could be crossed by using a causeway, though this was not without its hazards for men returning after a night on the town. In 1892 a guardhouse was built at Stamshaw, and, by 1900, a swing bridge had made the floating bridge redundant.

By Fisher's time, muzzle-loading cannon had been superseded by more sophisticated, heavier, breech-loaded guns that could send a conical shell thousands of yards with greater accuracy. This development brought with it a need for increasingly sophisticated technical skills and Fisher was instrumental in promoting a change in attitudes and practice. A visitor to *Excellent* in 1896 described some of the activities he witnessed:

> Our next visit is to see the heavy gun battery which may be described as the *pièce de résistance* of the island. Here in a shed some 600 feet long are to be found types of all the various guns in use in the navy … Round each gun is a class, in some cases working the gun with that dash and vigour that only the British bluejacket is capable of, in others having the gun or mounting described to them, whilst an armourers' class are stripping the mounting of a 4.7 inch quick-firer. As we pass down the battery we hear from various instructors a medley of orders of the sort: 'Inside the cylinder is a valve key which '…, 'Lie down!', 'Ten knots right

147 *(top)*
Barrack Room, HMS *Excellent*, c.1910.

148 *(above)*
Playing cards in Barrack Room, 1896.

149 *(right)*
Whale Island Bridge, c.1909.

150 *(left)*
Loading of 4-inch anti-aircraft gun at
Whale Island, 1930s.

151 *(below)*
Armourer's Workshop, 1896.

152 *(bottom)*
Electric Workshop, 1896.

WHALE ISLAND, PORTSMOUTH.

deflection …', 'Carry on!', 'Ten degrees of elevation …', until arriving at the north end we find a complete model of a casemate similar to those built in the Royal Sovereign and other ships to protect their auxiliary armament. As we leave the north end of the battery a succession of reports attract our attention and we espy a class at revolver practice in the pistol gallery, whilst in the distance some slight puffs of bluish haze point out to us where the rifle shooting practice is going on at Tipner rifle range, and an immense red flag flying from a hulk up the harbour, the Nettle, late Thunderer, whose many honourable scars testify to the warmth of the enemy's fire at Acre, shows us that an armour plate is being tested on board her by the experimental party.'[1]

Within the confines of Portsmouth Harbour, training men in the use of heavy guns was hazardous, so a small fleet of gunboats and the *Hero* were fitted out to train men in more realistic conditions on the open sea. This also went some way to avoiding complaints from Queen Victoria that the firing of heavy guns 'incommoded her when in residence at Osborne'.

Between the turn of the century and the First World War a number of revolutionary initiatives to improve marksmanship at sea were adopted, encouraged by Admiral Sir Percy Scott. Among them was the Dreyer Fire Control Table, a sophisticated device that mechanically computed variables, such as speed of ship, speed of target, range, wind force and direction, and delivered instructions to the gunners.

Scott also initiated the traditional Field Gun competition, a recent casualty of defence spending cuts. During the Boer War, Percy Scott landed his ship's guns in support of the Army during the siege of Ladysmith. The tough physical demands

153 *(top left)*
Ammunition instruction, 1896.

154 *(top)*
Taking cover in a shallow trench, 1896.

155 *(above)*
Ammunition Room.

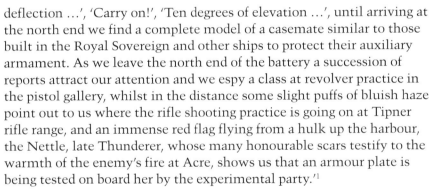

156 *(bottom left)*
A rolling motion platform simulates conditions at sea while trainees fire a 3 pdr gun.

157 *(below right)*
Acting Sub-Lieutenants' revolver training.

158 *(bottom right)*
6-inch gun ready for firing.

of dismantling, carrying and reassembling the guns, together with the team spirit it encouraged, were considered excellent training, and became a popular feature of the Royal Tournament.

During the First World War, the Experimental Department, which was concerned with gunnery and armour research and development, expanded to cope with the demands of war, and carried out gun trials in 1,206 different ships. Research into the ballistics of anti-aircraft gunnery was also initiated at *Excellent*, on a range at Eastney.

The Tipner rifle ranges were extended in 1900, and brick shelters and a cookhouse for musketry classes erected there in the 1910s. In 1919 the site of an RAF kite balloon station at Tipner was transferred to *Excellent* for use as an Anti-Gas School, though responsibility for its administration was passed to the RN Barracks seven years later.

During the Second World War gunnery training continued at *Excellent*, while an additional training range was opened at HMS *Blazer* at Bembridge (1943-6). Anti-aircraft training was carried out at Northern Parade School, HMS *Queen Charlotte* in Southport (1941-6) and HMS *St Barbara* on Bognor Regis Pier (1943-5). The latter was named after the Patron Saint of Artillerists, in whose name *Excellent*'s church was dedicated in 1934. Early in the war, the Experimental Department moved to Bordean House near Petersfield, a trial relocation in preparation for a move to Carlisle in the event of an enemy invasion along the

south coast. The department, which was busy adapting equipment to accommodate the new radar techniques, returned to Whale Island in 1942. The department expanded to cope with the testing and arming of landing and support craft in preparation for the D-Day landings.

In 1985 *Excellent* closed, its functions being absorbed by HMS *Nelson,* but a reorganisation in the mid-1990s led to its reopening as a complex training establishment comprising Whale Island, Horsea Island and Tipner Range. This includes the *Phoenix* School for Nuclear, Biological, Chemical Defence and Damage

159
Sham attack on Whale Island. These scenes are from a training display put on for the heads of colonial countries in 1907.
From left to right, top row: Two hundred men hauling a 4.7 gun up the slopes of the shore; landing on the shore; an armoured car played a minor role.
From left to right, bottom row: Men retreating to their boats; view from the defenders' position.

160 *(left)*
Loading of 6-inch gun.

161 *(below)*
An artist's depiction of a 6-inch gun
in action during the First World War.

Control, the RN Regulating School (discipline, law, security), the Naval Military
Training School (handling of small arms, anti-terrorist training) and the RN
School of Leadership and Management. Other tenant units include the adminis-
trative headquarters of the Royal Marines, sea cadets and the Defence Diving
School. The destroyer HMS *Bristol* is permanently moored off Whale Island and is
used as a training ship. Future planned transfers to the Island include the Fleet Air
Arm's headquarters and the navy's nerve centre currently based at Northwood.

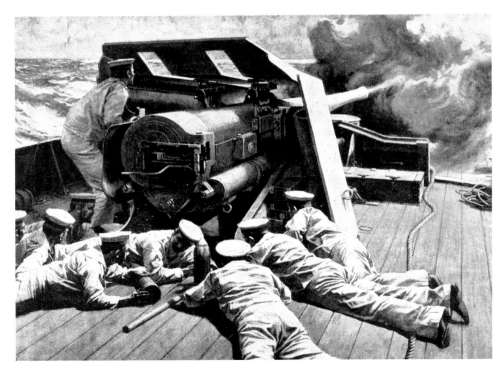

Chapter 9

UNDERWATER WARFARE
MINES, TORPEDOES AND SUBMARINES

162
Portsmouth-built submarine *K5*, which was lost with all hands at the mouth of the Channel in 1921. The majority of the 53 men who died were from Portsmouth.

In 1871 the army was given responsibility for the development and application of what became known as the 'torpedo', for coastal defence. These early weapons lacked any independent means of locomotion and were actually sea mines. There were two basic types, one was designed to explode when struck by a ship, and the other was set off by observers on the shore by means of an electric cable.

The first self-propelled torpedo had been invented in 1866 by Robert Whitehead, and the following year the naval gunnery school HMS *Excellent* set up a section to study and develop the new weapon, which offered greater flexibility and accuracy than the static 'torpedo' or sea mine.

The military responsibility for coastal sea-mining was originally a low-key affair based in Gillingham, but had expanded to five divisions by 1888, based at Gosport, Plymouth, the Thames, Milford Haven and the Severn. There was a concern that endowing this service with too much importance would suggest that the Royal Navy was incapable of defending British ports from attack, and it was not until the First World War that the potential of the sea mine was recognised and taken seriously.

In 1879 a mimic attack by enemy ships was staged off Gilkicker involving Royal Engineers, Marines and the Navy. Small explosive charges were used to prevent casualties, and military attachés of several foreign embassies were invited along to watch from Fort Monckton, presumably to demonstrate the folly of such incursions.[1]

In this year, Royal Engineers took over Fort Blockhouse as a sea-mining base, and new buildings and piers were erected. In 1884, the 4th Company (Gosport, Submarine Miners), with responsibility for the Portsmouth and Spithead area defence, moved into Fort Monckton. The fort, which had been built a hundred years earlier, had ceased to be part of the main defences. By the 1890s, coastal mining had become established and men were needed to train in the new science. A school was started at Monckton, where Royal Engineer recruits were trained as electricians and divers and instructed in the safe handling of chemicals and explosives. Training and testing of mines took place off Fort Gilkicker in Stokes Bay.[2]

By 1905 sea mining responsibility was passed to the Royal Navy and the trained miners from Monckton were dispersed to Royal Engineer units. The Royal Engineer School of Electric Lighting moved into the fort, where research and training took place in the development and use of searchlights for defence purposes.

163 *(left)*
Remote controlled mines activated by electric cables at Fort Monckton during training exercise in 1897.

164 *(right)*
Preparing mines at Fort Gilkicker, 1897.

165 *(below)*
Mines on the Mining Pier, Portsmouth Harbour, c.1897. (*St Vincent* is on the left.)

166 *(below right)*
Electric cable testing, 1897.

Monckton also reverted to its original function as the home of a fortress unit, the 4 (Fortress) Company Royal Engineers.

In naval hands, coastal mining appears to have suffered some neglect, with efforts being made to pass responsibility back to the army. But the U-Boat offensive of 1917, when horned mines were introduced, demonstrated their importance and effectiveness in modern warfare.

The first self-propelled torpedo, driven by compressed air, was operational by 1868. At the Navy's principal gunnery school, *Excellent*, Jacky Fisher recognised its potential, as he did of virtually every innovation of the era. He argued that a separate establishment, independent of *Excellent*, was needed to develop and train men in the new torpedo science. By now a Commander, Fisher was put in charge of the new Torpedo School, housed in a group of old wooden hulks centred on HMS *Vernon*, the instructional ship. Commissioned in 1876, *Vernon* was moored in Fountain Lake, close to the Dockyard. The hulk *Ariadne* provided accommodation, while *Actaeon* served as a workshop. Other ships were added, including the *Donegal*, *Marlborough* and *Warrior*. A Torpedo Depot comprising workshops and store buildings was built in Portsmouth Dockyard in 1886, though this became

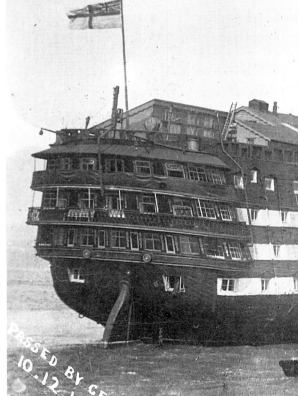

167 *(top)*
Group of Royal Engineer officers at
Fort Monckton, *c.*1897. (Left to right:
Major Aylmer-Jones, Captain
Hawley, Lieutenant Yockney, and
2nd Lieutenants Mortimer and
Buckley.)

168 *(above)*
Mine-laying vessel in Stokes Bay,
*c.*1897.

169 *(top right)*
Training of electricians, *c.*1897.

independent from *Vernon* and was relocated to Frater in 1959. Between 1885 and 1889, a massive torpedo range was constructed by the joining together of Great and Little Horsea Island using convict labour and thousands of tons of chalk from Paulsgrove chalk-pit.

By 1895, the busy Fountain Lake had become unsuitable as a mooring, and *Vernon* was moved to Portchester Creek where she remained until the transfer ashore to the vacated Gunwharf site in 1923.

Apart from its instructional role, *Vernon* had three experimental departments: Whitehead (torpedo), Mining and Electrical. The attached Vernon Flotilla, comprising destroyers and trawlers, was employed in practical running and testing of torpedoes and mines. Use of the Horsea Torpedo Range declined as the speed and range of torpedoes increased, requiring a longer test range than Horsea could offer. As a result, trials were conducted in Stokes Bay, where the pier and its cranes were used for preparation and test runs. Stokes Bay Torpedo Experimental Station came under the command of *Vernon* in 1921, but by the early 1930s, the bay was used solely for aircraft torpedo tests, with surface torpedo test runs being moved to Weymouth.

The Mining Department had been transferred ashore during the First World War, before the other functions of *Vernon*, and was responsible for mining,

170 *(left)*
The Torpedo School, HMS *Vernon*, in Portsmouth Harbour, *c*.1915.

171 *(below)*
Main entrance to HMS *Vernon*, 1965.

172 *(above)*
Robotic caricature of a Seaman
Torpedoman published in
Portsmouth as a postcard, *c*.1910.

173 *(above right)*
Main workshop at HMS *Vernon*,
c.1910.

174 *(below)*
Torpedoes on display in Portsmouth.

minesweeping and countermeasures, such as paravanes. A separate Mine Depot was built at Frater in 1918 for the servicing, storage and distribution of mines to the Fleet.

The Electrical Department developed searchlights, telephones, batteries and switchgear, while another department, established in 1927, carried out research into chemical warfare.

During the 1930s, *Vernon* was responsible for the development of Motor Torpedo Boats, though this was transferred to HMS *Hornet* at Gosport at the beginning of the Second World War. Work continued on the development of advanced mines, and countermeasures began to be considered, based on intelligence reports of German technological advances in magnetic mines. But ships were being sunk in large numbers off the east coast, and it was not until the principle of operation was established after an intact mine was recovered off Shoeburyness that effective countermeasures were researched at *Vernon* and put into practice.[3] A specialised mine-disposal team was on call to make safe increasingly sophisticated unexploded land and sea mines all over the country, and return them to *Vernon* for examination.

175 *(above)*
HMS *Vernon* Officers' Quarters,
c.1935.

176 *(right)*
Stokes Bay Torpedo Experimental
Station, *c*.1930.

Air raids on Portsmouth prompted the temporary removal of sections of *Vernon* to less vulnerable locations, including West Leigh House, Hinxman's Garage (Fareham), Hillside House (Purbrook), Alverstoke, and Roedean School (near Brighton). The Mine Design Department (a separate, civilian, Admiralty establishment, located in the base) was moved to Leigh Park House, where engineers and scientists designed mines for underwater sabotage attacks and for dropping by Bomber Command in enemy harbours.

Over two-thirds of enemy shipping casualties caused by British action were attributed to either the mine or torpedo, and more than 900 U-Boats were sunk at sea, reflecting the importance of the research, development and training carried out at *Vernon*.

In 1945, the base underwent reorganisation and its functions were broadened to encompass the training of men in virtually all aspects of underwater warfare, and the conduct of sea trials of all new weapons and devices. These ranged from a new coastal minesweeper to a valve in a diving suit. For the first time, diving was included in the training, and use was made of the familiar landmark mining tower built in 1921. Eleven tenders were also used for sea training in diving, minesweeping, mine-laying, and torpedoes.

Large areas of *Vernon* were devastated during the air raids of 1941, and many temporary huts were used until a rebuilding plan was started in 1954. *Vernon* ceased to exist as an independent establishment in 1986, though the site continued to be used by various units. One, the Portsmouth Area Clearance Diving Unit, was responsible for defusing old torpedoes and bombs that were washed up on the coast between the Humber and Swanage.[4]

The early Royal Engineer miners constructed a number of piers and jetties at Fort Blockhouse which were to prove useful when the Admiralty took over the fort in 1905 and established the Royal Navy's first Submarine Boat Station. The location was ideal as Haslar Creek was deep enough and there was room for expansion. Admiral Jacky Fisher, now First Sea Lord, recognised the destructive

177 *(top)*
Submarine *A5* shortly after its launch in 1904.

178 *(above)*
Admiral Sir John (Jacky) Fisher, First Sea Lord, *c.*1905.

179 *(left)*
The submarine base at Fort Blockhouse, *c.*1910.

180 *(below left)*
A submarine taking in ammunition, *c.*1925.

181 *(below right)*
U-Boats at Portsmouth Dockyard after the surrender of the German Fleet in 1918.

potential of the submarine, but his fellow admirals were less keen, describing them as 'underhand, unfair and damned un-English'. HMS *Dolphin* and HMS *Mercury*, two old hulks, were attached to the base which had few of the amenities expected of naval barracks. Officers are said to have felt aggrieved that their quarters at the fort were converted stables, a feeling no doubt made worse that they were engaged in duties that were considered 'no occupation for a gentleman'. The early submarines were primitive and there were a series of tragic accidents. Two fatal accidents occurred in the busy Solent waters near the Nab. In 1904 the *A1* was struck by a passing liner and sunk with the loss of 11 men, and in 1912 the *A3* came into collision with a torpedo gunboat with the loss of 14 lives. These were particularly poignant incidents, with a great public sense of uncertainty and fear over the manner of the mens' deaths. Local relief funds were started to raise money for bereaved families, and when they were eventually retrieved the bodies were buried in Haslar Cemetery.[5]

By the outbreak of the First World War, Britain had 77 submarines, and though they were safer and more reliable than before, only a handful were able to travel more than a hundred miles. But the submarine as a machine of war was to gain the public seal of approval following the exploits of Lt. Commander Norman Holbrook, who became a local and national hero in December 1914 when he dived his submarine *B11* under the minefields of the Dardanelles and sank a Turkish cruiser.[6]

In 1924 the old hulk, HMS *Dolphin*, was sold off and the name transferred to the shore establishment, which served as the main training base for submariners and the base for an operational squadron. The base outgrew the confines of Blockhouse, and an area of Nissen Huts was built which served as accommodation during the Second World War. At this time the fort was armed with an assortment of anti-aircraft and machine guns, the latter manned by Royal Marines.[7] Submarines based at *Dolphin* continued to be used for specialised training, but following the heavy air raids of 1941, it was decided to transfer the main part to Blyth. Submarines were also used to land agents in Nazi-occupied Europe, while submersible two-man Chariots, which were developed on Horsea Island and tested at *Dolphin*, carried out sabotage raids on enemy harbours. Two midget *X*-craft submarines were sent to carry out reconnaissance in preparation for the D-Day landings.

By the 1970s, the First Submarine Squadron based at *Dolphin* comprised eight submarines that were operational at any given time, mainly on patrol far from home. The training school consisted of three buildings near the base of the Submarine Escape Training Tank, a 100 foot high tower used to train 3,500 submariners from all over the world in the techniques of escape.

In 1996 the submarine training school was transferred to HMS *Raleigh* at Torpoint, Cornwall, and HMS *Dolphin* was decommissioned in September 1998, when Fort Blockhouse became the headquarters of the tri-service Royal Defence Medical College and 33 Field Hospital.[8] The training tank, however, remains operational having been considered too expensive to move.

182
Submarine *Unity* entering Portsmouth Harbour in 1938, shortly after its launch.

Chapter 10

DEFENCE IN THE AIR

183
Demonstration of the new
hydroplane by pilot Commander
Samson during the Naval Display
at Spithead in 1912.

In 1911, the *Portsmouth Times* reported the visit of the first aeroplane to the area.[1] The pilot was a Mr. Gilmour, who flew his frail aircraft over Fort Blockhouse where his brother was stationed. As a joke he bombed him with oranges, an inadvertent recognition, perhaps, of the potential of the new flying machine. A solitary attack on Portsmouth by Zeppelin *L31* in the First World War proved harmless, due in large part to the efforts of the men manning the coastal guns and searchlights, who forced the airship to fly at a height that prevented accurate bombing. But forty years after Mr. Gilmour had taken off from Haslar recreation ground to the cheers of an awe-struck crowd, Portsmouth and Gosport were being blitzed. By the end of the Second World War, 1,041 civilians in Portsmouth and Gosport had been killed and one in ten homes made uninhabitable or destroyed.

Some of the earliest attempted flights with gliders were conducted by enthusiastic amateurs. Locally, these brief flights were made on land near Fort Monckton and later at Grange Camp Field (a site between Forts Rowner and Grange) by members of Portsmouth Aero Club, which was formed in 1909. Naval interest in aviation began when two submariners, Lieutenants Porte and Pirie, designed and built a glider at Fort Blockhouse. The fragile construction was towed in a boat up the harbour to Paulsgrove, launched off Portsdown Hill and wrecked. Further pioneering experiments were carried out by Gosport submariners at Portchester and Grange Camp Field.

In 1912, Grange was one of five sites chosen by the newly formed Royal Flying Corps to become a military airfield, and by 1914 the ground had been made level for the first squadron. Forts Grange and Rowner were taken over in 1914 and 1915, the displaced Royal Garrison Artillery being moved to Fort Brockhurst, Portsdown Hill and Purbrook.

On the outbreak of war, Gosport's first squadron was immediately sent to France to support the British Expeditionary Force, and has the distinction of having the first aeroplane to be shot down. Meanwhile the Admiralty set up two new Royal Naval Air Service squadrons, one based at Grange being put under the command of Arthur Longmore, who led a daring bombing raid on U-Boats at Antwerp in 1915. In the same year the first Zeppelin attacks on Britain took place, and though little damage was done, the airship was seen as an effective threat as a weapon of terror. The Gosport squadron was relocated to Dunkirk, from which it carried out bombing raids on Zeppelin bases. Pilots were also trained to ward off Zeppelin raiders over England.

The tragic deaths of many young airmen – known as 'Fokker fodder' – in the battle over the trenches of the Somme was witnessed at first hand by Major Smith-Barry, who established the School of Flying at Grange to train pilots how to get out of trouble, rather than simply to avoid it. Innovations included dual controls for pilot and pupil, and the 'Gosport Tube' which enabled the observer and pilot to talk to each other. This device was adopted by air forces throughout the war and was in use up until the 1940s.

The rivalry between the military and naval wings of the Royal Flying Corps was a major factor in the formation of the independent Royal Air Force in 1918. In the same year, a special squadron was formed at Gosport which had responsibility for the testing of and training in torpedo dropping techniques. Flights took place over Stokes Bay where the pier served as an outstation of the Torpedo School, HMS *Vernon*.

In the 1910s the navy conducted its first 'hydroplane' flights, and in 1912 held a display at Spithead to convince an assembled group of Members of Parliament of its usefulness in reconnaissance. An enthusiastic reporter described the scene:

> The air seemed full of these sweeping naval birds. Then the first came with a swoop right over the heads of gazing seamen and senators. Then an excited cry, 'He's alighting' from all mouths. Yes, now he is touching the water, and clouds of fine spray are dashing up high in the air. The aviator rests for a while and then is off again, skimming over the waves, hither and thither. Soon he turns into the wind and with his engine whirring at full speed rises for a moment. 'He's off now.' 'No, no.' 'Yes, he's up,' cry the spectators as again the hydroplane is soaring through the air, the water dripping from the shining floats. It was a great moment.[2]

The demonstration evidently did the trick. The following year the naval wing of the Royal Flying Corps set up a seaplane

184 *(above)*
Crowds in awe of the new hydroplane on Southsea Beach, 1912.

185 *(top right)*
Fairey IIId aircraft inside Slip Gate at *Daedalus* in the 1920s.

186 *(bottom right)*
Fairey IIIf on the beach at Lee-on-Solent in the early 1930s. The Fairey IIIf was the most widely used aeroplane in the Fleet Air Arm between the wars, and was used to train observers at Lee.

training base at Calshot. With the outbreak of war, Calshot's seaplanes patrolled the Channel looking for enemy submarines. They went armed with bombs which the pilots kept on their laps and tossed out at the appropriate moment, a hit or miss affair with few hits.

During the spring of 1917, the U-Boat offensive was having a devastating impact on British shipping. This was countered by a number of measures, including sending ships out in convoys, and by the introduction of new technology, including sonar detection, depth charges and paravanes. More patrol seaplanes were built with bomb racks and primitive but effective bomb sights. This created a desperate demand for trained crew that the Calshot base could not cope with. Lee-on-the-Solent was chosen as a stop-gap measure until another more permanent base could be established at Holy Island off the Northumbrian coast. The gentle sloping beach at Lee and the shelter provided by the Isle of Wight made it an ideal temporary

location, though lifting gear had to be used to haul the seaplanes to the sea until slipways were cut. Canvas hangars and a tent encampment were erected on the western side of Lee, while officers were billeted in the town and at Warsash. The Naval Seaplane Training School was opened in July 1917 and plans for the Holy Island base were scrapped a few months later.

By the end of the war the base had expanded to accommodate over 800 personnel and 69 seaplanes, and the Royal Naval Air Service and the Royal Flying Corps were amalgamated to form the Royal Air Force. Between the wars the name of the base was changed a number of times until the Royal Navy resumed control of the Fleet Air Arm in 1937, and recommissioned it as HMS *Daedalus* in 1939. The airfield was enlarged and was in operational use throughout the Second World War, except for a temporary closure due to enemy bombing during the Battle of Britain when three hangars and 42 aircraft were destroyed. Eight Wrens were killed in their billet during another attack. RAF fighters used the airfield and a large number of WAAFs served on the ground, servicing aircraft and repairing and packing parachutes. On D-Day alone, 335 sorties were flown from the airfield to clear the skies above Normandy.

Famous names who were based at *Daedalus* during the war years included Laurence Olivier, taking time off between *Wuthering Heights* and the patriotic

187 *(far left)*
Blackburn Darts over the Solent, *c.*1925. This aircraft was used to teach torpedo-dropping techniques.

188 *(above)*
Westland Wasps at Fleetlands, *c.*1970. The Wasp was a light anti-submarine strike helicopter, which operated from small ships and carried two Mk 44 homing torpedoes.

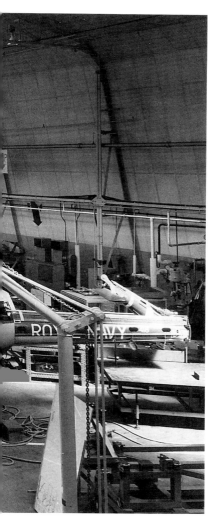

Henry V, and Lieutenant-Commander Ralph Richardson, who commented after the war that Olivier and himself probably held the record for pranged aircraft at *Daedalus*. Richardson made amends by boosting the morale of troops during personal appearances, including the opening of the British Restaurant for servicemen in Havant in 1942.

After the war came a number of changes in use, and in 1958 it became the Fleet Air Arm's main technical training establishment, renamed HMS *Ariel*. The name *Daedalus* was reinstated in 1965, and the Air Engineering School reformed by the amalgamation with HMS *Condor*. The Inter-Service Hovercraft Unit was also established here, making use of the former seaplane slipway facing Cowes where much of the pioneering hovercraft work was carried out. Other units based here included the Naval Air Trials Installation Unit, the Mobile Aircraft Repair, Transport and Salvage Unit, and the Air Medical and Survival School at Seafield Park. The Search and Rescue flight was formed at *Daedalus* in 1973, with three Wessex Mark V helicopters, and covered 170 miles of Britain's busiest coastline from Sussex to Devon.

The base closed in 1996 and its various functions dispersed, with the Air Engineering School moving to HMS *Sultan* in Gosport. A memorial to the officers and men of the Fleet Air Arm who died in the Second World War remains, overlooking the Solent.

Between the wars, Fort Grange Airfield continued as an important RAF training establishment for pilots and air crew, but by the Second World War it had become too small to cope with more modern aircraft. Nevertheless, it was used as an emergency landing strip for battle-damaged aircraft, including several Flying Fortresses during the D-Day operations. In 1945 it was taken over by the navy, renamed HMS *Siskin* and used as a base for helicopter squadrons. It also trained aircraft handlers for carriers and continued its role in torpedo development. In 1956, torpedo development was transferred to Culdrose in Cornwall and Gosport Airfield was closed. The Rowner naval housing estate comprising 3,000 married quarters was built on the western part of the airfield, while the eastern side was taken by the Naval Marine Engineering School, HMS *Sultan*. In 1970 the Naval Pay Records Computer Centre, HMS *Centurion*, opened in the north-eastern corner of the site.

Work began on the construction of Fleetlands Aircraft Repair Yard (RNARY) on the eve of the Second World War on Admiralty property to the north-west of Bedenham Armament Depot. Building was interrupted by heavy enemy bombing, but in 1941 the first aircraft, a Swordfish, was received for repair. By 1942 the civilian workforce numbered 1,100, most of who were trainees. Aircraft in need of repair were ferried up Portsmouth Harbour on lighters to Foxbury Point. Over eight hundred women were eventually employed in the workshops, with repairs being stringently checked by specialised inspectors.[3]

The post-war jet age saw the introduction of the Sea Hawk and Sea Venom. During this time repaired aircraft were transported by road to *Daedalus* for flight testing. The last fixed-wing aircraft to be repaired at Fleetlands was a Scimitar in 1967. The following year the yard became a repair centre for helicopters,

189
Aerial view of Fleetlands, showing Westland Whirlwinds at Foxbury Point, c.1957.

developing into the largest such facility in Europe. All types of military and naval helicopters have been repaired and serviced in the hangars and workshops on the 127 acre site, including Wessex, Whirlwinds, Wasps, Sea Kings and Lynx.

Following reorganisation in 1998, Fleetlands is now part of the Defence Aviation Repair Agency. The Wessex Mk 5 helicopter on permanent display outside its main gate was involved in the rescue of men from the Royal Fleet Auxiliary ship *Sir Galahad* during the Falklands War.[4]

Like many private companies, Airspeed's factory off the Eastern Road was put into service for the war effort at the outbreak, though it had been supplying RAF trainer planes for several years. The company had been started in 1931 when Nevil S. Norway and Hessell Tiltman built a monoplane in a shed in Leeds. They moved to an old bus garage in York, and then went into mass production at a purpose-built factory in Portsmouth. In July 1940, it became the first British aircraft factory to be bombed, closely followed by the Supermarine (Spitfire) Works at Southampton. Airspeed resumed production and became best known for the Horsa military glider, which played an active role in operations in Arnhem, Norway, Italy and the liberation of Europe. After the war, the former managing director blended technical description with human drama as the popular novelist, Nevil Shute.

In 2001 the government announced plans to transfer the Fleet Air Arm's headquarters to Whale Island, reviving the area's traditional links with naval air defence.

Chapter 11

Naval Communication, Navigation and Radar

190
The first Semaphore Tower, Old
Portsmouth.

Before the introduction of the telegraph in 1847, communication between Portsmouth and the Admiralty in London was achieved using a chain of signalling stations. The first local stations were built in around 1795 on Southsea Common and
Portsdown Hill, with messages conveyed using a shutter system taking up to
twenty minutes to arrive.[1] By 1817 this system had been superseded by the semaphore system using a post and two arms, the positions of which, relative to the
vertical post indicated a letter of the alphabet. The first semaphore tower was built
in 1817 on the Square Tower, at the bottom of the High Street near the Port Admiral's residence. By 1833 the Port Admiral had moved into the Dockyard and a new
tower was erected straddling the Sail Loft and Rigging House. The last semaphore
message was sent from this 120 ft. wooden structure on the last day of 1847, when
the electric telegraph was introduced. The semaphore arms were removed but the
tower remained until it was destroyed by fire in 1913. The current tower, which is
much the same design as the previous one, was constructed in stone in the late
1920s. The old Lion Gate, dating from the 1770s, was incorporated into the design
beneath the tower, and renamed 'The Gateway of Empire', symbolising the role of
the Navy in acquiring and maintaining the British Empire.[2] Communication between ships by semaphore continued into the second half of the 20th century,
along with flag signalling which was taught at the Signal School on HMS *Victory*
in the Harbour.

The first wireless telegraph message across the English Channel was sent by
Marconi in 1899, and the potential for naval communication was recognised by
the Admiralty who adopted his system in the same year. Developmental responsibility was given to HMS *Vernon*, then a floating establishment moored in Portsmouth Harbour. By the end of 1900, the Royal Navy had 32 Marconi sets and 19
other sets manufactured at *Vernon*. The old HMS *Warrior*, a hulk that served as

part of *Vernon*, was rigged out with wireless equipment and by 1906 a range of 1,000 miles had been achieved. In 1907 plans were made by the Admiralty to establish three wireless telegraphy stations at Gibraltar, Cleethorpes and Horsea Island. The station at Horsea was completed in 1909, with electric power being supplied by the generator in Portsmouth Dockyard via a cable under the Harbour. Just before the First World War three 446 ft. wooden masts were erected by Navy ratings and riggers from the Dockyard. These were superseded in 1933 by steel towers less than half their size. The station ceased operation in about 1960.

In 1906, the Signal School was set up in the newly built Royal Naval Barracks. Recruits were trained in electric telegraphy, electric light and heliography, before qualifying as signalmen. During the First World War, staff from the *Vernon*, who had responsibility for the development of new methods of communication, were transferred to the School, and new buildings were erected on the parade ground to accommodate them. Wrens were employed in the testing of valves during the war. Thermionic valves and direction finding were developed by the Experimental Department, and, in 1928, it was an officer of the department who first identified the possibility of what later became known as radar – the detection of objects using radio waves. From 1935 staff were engaged on this 'magic eye' research and, three years later, the first seaborne radar sets were fitted in HMS *Sheffield* and HMS *Rodney*. An aircraft flying at 3,000 ft. could be detected at a range of thirty miles using these experimental sets. With the outbreak of war, radar development became a priority. Parts of the department were moved to Eastney Fort East, a disused school in Onslow Road, Commercial Chambers (in what is now Lord Montgomery Way), Southsea Castle and Nutbourne.

New defensive and offensive applications were designed – surface warning and gunnery ranging. The introduction of rotating aerials enabled the monitoring of echoes around 360 degrees. Revolutionary micro-wave equipment was also developed and successfully used in ships and aircraft to detect enemy submarines.

The devastating air raids on the city in 1941 prompted an almost total evacuation of staff. The training side was relocated to Leydene House at West Meon

191
The original Semaphore Tower above the Sail Loft and Rigging House, *c*.1910.

(which remained there and became a separate establishment, HMS *Mercury*), while much of the Experimental Unit went to Lythe Hill House in Haslemere, where Nissen huts were erected on the estate. This became the headquarters of the renamed Admiralty Signal Establishment, which by now employed over 1,000 staff at 26 locations all over the country. In 1948 (and with a careful eye on the acronym) it was renamed the Admiralty Signal and Radar Establishment, and in the same year moved into a prominent, purpose-built complex on Portsdown Hill. Plans for the Main Block were condemned by some local people because of the effect on the skyline, though the Admiralty recruited the Fine Arts Commission to endorse its design and position.

After an amalgamation with the Admiralty Gunnery Establishment, and with the development of guided missiles, another name was adopted by which it became most familiarly known – the Admiralty Surface Weapons Establishment, or ASWE.

The need for naval lieutenants to be trained in navigational duties in Jacky Fisher's new navy led to the setting up of a Navigation School in 1903. This was originally based on an old cruiser, *Mercury*, which soon proved too small, and the school moved into the old Royal Naval College in the south-east corner of the Dockyard in 1905. Additional courses in pilotage and watchkeeping were run, and the school was renamed HMS *Dryad* after one of the torpedo-gunboat tenders which was used.

The school remained in the old building until it was badly damaged in an air raid in 1941, during which the neighbouring Admiralty House was also hit. *Dryad* was moved out of

192 *(above)*
Signalling at sea by semaphore, *c*.1925.

193 *(right)*
The end of the wooden Semaphore Tower in a fire in 1913. This was attributed to German spies and arsonistic suffragettes but is more likely to have been an accident.

194
Admiralty Surface Weapons
Establishment Main Block on
Portsdown Hill.

Portsmouth to the safety of Southwick House, a grand Victorian mansion chosen by the Commander-in-Chief, Admiral Sir William James, who regularly went pheasant shooting on the Southwick Estate.

In 1944 the Navigation School was temporarily moved out of Southwick to Greenwich so that the house could be used as a base by the Supreme Allied Commander, General Eisenhower, General Montgomery, and other military, air and naval commanders who planned and launched the historic invasion of Normandy from there. *Dryad* returned shortly afterwards, and has remained at Southwick to this day. With the introduction of radar and other technologies in the Second World War, the Navigation and Fighter Direction branches of the Royal Navy were combined, laying the foundations for the School of Maritime Operations. Meanwhile, HMS *Mercury* at Leydene House, West Meon, took on the role of a combined Navigation and Signals School until its closure in 1993.

Chapter 12

Naval Barracks and Other Establishments

The 'General Depot'

With the abandonment of the press gangs at the end of the Napoleonic Wars, the navy experienced a manning problem exacerbated by the notoriously bad living conditions on board the hulks in Portsmouth Harbour. These old wooden ships included the *Marlborough*, the *Asia*, the *Duke of Wellington* and the *Hannibal*, and were known collectively as the 'General Depot'. They acted as barracks for seamen, but were dark, cold, poorly ventilated and had no facilities for men to wash themselves or their clothes. An exception was the *Bellerophon*, which was fitted out as a model hulk and was less uncomfortable than the others. This gesture made little difference and the service continued to experience severe problems in attracting new recruits and preventing men leaving. These insanitary hulks were 'the curse of the navy', according to Admiral Sir Charles Napier,[1] but it took nearly fifty years for the curse to be lifted.

Royal Naval Barracks

From 1858 onwards, suggestions were made for permanent barracks to be built in and around the Dockyard, but it was not until 1899 that construction began in Portsea on a 100 acre site occupied by the Anglesea Barracks, Convict Prison wardens' quarters and Military Hospital. The Admiralty arranged for a replacement military hospital to be built on the slopes of Portsdown Hill (Alexandra Royal) to free up the site on the south side of Queen Street for new officers' quarters. Some Anglesea Barrack buildings were retained and converted, with room for 4,000 men sleeping in hammocks in four rows extending the length of the many long barrack rooms.

The Royal Naval Barracks was opened on 30 September 1903, when officers and ratings vacated the hulks and marched out of the Dockyard and along Queen Street to their new quarters. The *Hampshire Telegraph* described the new accommodation as 'a perfect palace ... with electric light, lavatories on each floor and water taps in every room ...'.[2]

From December 1903, cap bands were issued in the name of HMS *Victory*, leading to some confusion with Nelson's flagship which was moored in Portsmouth Harbour at the time. This confusion continued until 1974 when the name was changed to HMS *Nelson*.

In 1906 the national press carried graphic accounts of 'a mutinous outbreak' at the barracks which was 'unparalleled in the modern history of our navy'.[3] An insensitive Gunnery Officer had succeeded in insulting and provoking several hundred stokers to riot, leading to many injuries and broken windows in the officers' quarters.

195 *(top left)*
Skeleton Crews comprising Sailors and Royal Marines, parading for inspection in Portsmouth Dockyard, *c.*1895.

196 *(left)*
Admiralty inspection in Portsmouth Dockyard, *c.*1903.

197 *(above)*
Royal Naval Barracks Main Gate, *c.*1905.

198 *(right)*
Officers' Quarters, *c.*1909.

199 *(below right)*
Stokers' Block, *c.*1916.

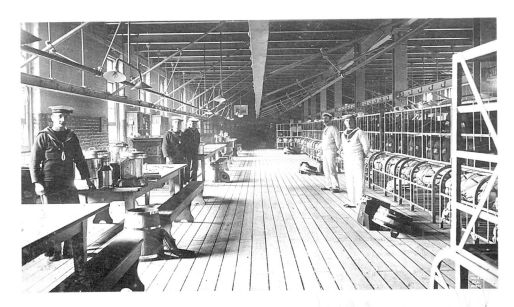

200 *(above)*
Mess Room, *c.*1912.

201 *(right)*
View looking across RN Barracks
Parade Ground, *c.*1905.

202 *(below)*
Instructional Battery, *c.*1910.

203 *(below right)*
Maxim Battery, *c.*1910.

The Navy's Paymaster

One of the primary causes of discontent on the lower deck that precipitated the Naval Mutiny at Spithead in 1797 was low pay. Not only had seamen's pay been frozen for 150 years, but also the arrangements for payment reduced its value further. Often, deductions halved its already meagre value, it was often paid over two years in arrears, and when it was paid in full it was in the form of tickets which had to be exchanged for cash at the ship's port of commission. This inevitably involved a further payment of a large percentage. By the time of Nelson's death, wages had been increased, though an ordinary seaman still received less than a soldier.[4] He did not fare much better in the Victorian Navy, though wage tickets were abolished and he was paid regularly in cash. Between the world wars, pay was increased and allowances for families, kit and victuals were introduced, though proposals to cut wages in 1931 prompted a refusal to put to sea at Invergordon.

The administration that handled the pay accounts, pensions, drafting and allotments of the post-war Navy were brought together at HMS *Centurion* in Rowner, Gosport, in 1970. It was the first large-scale naval establishment to be commissioned since the First World War and incorporated many functions formerly based at Bath, Haslemere and Reading, but also included the Royal Marines' pay accounts department from Eastney Barracks. Building work began on part of the old Grange Airfield in 1967 and its advanced £500,000 computer took several years before becoming fully operational. Amid reassurances that drafting would not be 'in the hands of a robot', the Naval Pay, Drafting and Records Establishment was launched with a complement of 500 staff in October 1970, handling the affairs of some 70,000 naval personnel.[5]

By 1998 the handling of pay, pensions and administration services for all armed forces was privatised, and the contract awarded to a US company.

Haslar Gunboat Yard

Haslar Gunboat Yard was built during the Crimean War to help repair and maintain the vast fleet of Victorian gunboats that was being built at that time. A model of it is believed to have appeared in the Great Exhibition of 1851. Building work began on Haslar Farm on the northern shore of Haslar peninsula in 1856 and the 20 covered sheds were completed the following year. By 1859 the yard was handling about fifty gunboats which were hauled up the slips by a steam-driven wheeled platform called a 'traverser' (known to workers there as 'the elephant'), which was capable of moving loads of up to 160 tons. This ingenious system was designed by the famous Portsmouth-born engineer, Isambard Kingdom Brunel, and served through both world wars, when torpedo and patrol boats were fitted out and repaired there. An electrically operated transporter was installed in 1952. By the 1970s, about 75 vessels a year were being repaired or refitted, including inshore minesweepers, harbour launches and fast patrol boats. The Yard's remoteness from the Dockyard, of which it was a part, together with the opening of the new Haslar Bridge led to its closure in 1978.

The Admiralty Experimental Works

The Admiralty Experimental Works was moved into the Gunboat Yard in 1886 by Robert Froude, whose father, William, had pioneered the use of paraffin wax models of ship's hulls to predict performance. These tests had taken place in a purpose-built tank in Torquay, where William Froude was commissioned by the Admiralty and encouraged by Isambard Kingdom Brunel.

After William Froude's death in 1879, his son persuaded the Admiralty that a larger testing vessel was necessary, and a concrete water tank was built at Haslar that measured 400 ft. long, 20 ft. wide and up to 9 ft. deep, nearly twice the length of the Torquay canal. A mahogany travelling carriage was set on rails above the tank from which a scale model was suspended, and the speed and resistance, or drag, recorded. Models of the hull of the *Dreadnought* were tested here before the revolutionary warship was built in the Dockyard. Launched in 1906, it was to prove faster than any other ship that preceded it, as well as being bigger and better armed. The introduction of turbine machinery was made possible by the adoption of small, high-speed propellers running astern, based on Froude's recommendations.

Work began on torpedo hydrodynamics in 1883, submarine design in 1904 and, during the First World War, hydroplanes and the anti-mine device, the paravane, were being tested. A wavemaker was installed in 1903 to allow tests in rough water. By the time Robert Froude retired in 1919, he had overseen nearly 200,000 tests, and, with his father, had made a major contribution to the efficiency and safety of the Navy's vessels. Their authoritative research and equipment was used as a model throughout the world.

Between the wars, tests were carried out on manoeuvrability, especially of destroyers, using Horsea Lake. A second ship tank was built in 1930-2, and during the Second World War they were used to carry out model tests on prototypes of the pre-fabricated Mulberry Harbours used to provide landing facilities for troops, vessels and equipment during the D-Day landings.

The original tank was extended in 1957 and a manoeuvring tank installed in 1960. Tests continued on propeller design, roll stabilisation, anchor design, and the behaviour of hulls in rough weather. In recent years, oil companies have sponsored research into the performance of offshore oil and gas platforms.

The work at Haslar was complemented by research and development carried out in the Central Dockyard Laboratory on materials, as well as an outstation at Eastney that was used primarily for the observation of sea trials in the Solent. Froude's original tank was closed in November 1993, though work continues at Haslar under the Defence Evaluation and Research Agency (DERA). This agency was formed in 1995 after a decision was taken to consolidate research and technology departments of the Ministry of Defence. With the decline of the defence industries, DERA is increasingly engaged in developing, applying and selling its technological expertise to private industry.

HMS *Phoenix*

HMS *Phoenix* formed at Tipner in 1946 from the Anti-Gas School on the site of what had been, at the end of the First World War, an RAF kite balloon station.[6] *Phoenix* became the Naval Atomic Biological Chemical Defence School, but was renamed the Nuclear Biological Chemical Defence School in 1964. Control of the school transferred to *Excellent* (as Phoenix NBCD School) and, from 1985, to *Nelson*. Loss of life during the Falklands War led to a large investment in fire fighting training, conducted on Horsea Island until a move to new facilities on Whale Island, took place in 2001.[7] The *Phoenix* school, once again part of *Excellent*, trains more than 12,000 men and women a year to cope with emergencies at sea.

HMS *Hornet*

A Coastal Motor Boat (CMB) base was in operation beside Haslar Bridge during the First World War, though it was not until 1921 that a permanent base was established, having moved from Osea Island on the Blackwater. In 1925 it adopted the name HMS *Hornet*. The following year it was taken over by HMS *Dolphin* and used by the RAF as a marine craft base until 1938. Meanwhile, at HMS *Vernon*, trials were taking place of the new Motor Torpedo Boat which innovative local shipbuilder Vosper was developing. With the outbreak of war, *Hornet* was reborn as a base for the new craft, and the distinctive roar of their powerful engines as they went on night patrols became familiar in the harbour area during the war. Fort Blockhouse was taken over to accommodate boat crews as *Hornet* expanded, forty of its motor launches and MTBs also being berthed at Dolphin.

Coastal Forces, of which *Hornet* was a part, had a low status within the Navy and was nicknamed 'costly farces', its small, light boats dubbed 'flying bedpans'. It was not until Motor Torpedo Boats worked together with powerful Motor Gun Boats in some daring actions against German convoys that Coastal Forces important role was recognised by the Admiralty.

After the war, *Hornet* was responsible for developing and conducting sea trials of new designs of Fast Patrol Boats and their weaponry, but, by 1957, the decision was made to close the base. It reopened as the Hornet Naval Yacht Centre in 1964, but is now the Joint Services Adventurous Sail Training Centre.

HMS *Sultan*

HMS *Sultan*, the Royal Naval Marine Engineering School, was established in 1956 on the site of Gosport Airfield (which had been renamed HMS *Siskin* in 1945). *Sultan* took its name from one of the earliest ironclads which was moored off Portsmouth Dockyard and served as the headquarters for engineering training up until the Second World War, when its functions were transferred ashore to Flathouse. By 1955, these premises had become inadequate and machinery and equipment was gradually transferred to the spacious workshops, offices and hangars of Gosport Airfield.[8] New facilities were installed and courses introduced to meet the increasingly technical and complex demands of the modern, post-war navy. These included the use of engine control simulators and courses in nuclear

204 *(above)*
Anti-gas class (Anson) at Tipner in 1926.

205 *(left)*
Fire-fighting training on Horsea Island, 1991.

206 *(below)*
Coastal Motor Boat base personnel at Haslar, 1919.

powered engines. Following reorganisation, *Sultan* is now the Royal Navy's Marine and Air Engineering School.

HMS *Collingwood*

Collingwood opened as a new entry training establishment for RN reservists in 1940 to cope with the demands of war. Sited south of Fort Fareham on 200 acres of farmland which had once been described as 'the best snipe marsh in the country', it grew from a handful of huts to the Navy's largest shore establishment, accommodating and training thousands of men and WRNS.

Collingwood's location away from the sea did not appear to compromise training. Within a year of its opening, the Commander-in-Chief at Portsmouth, Admiral Sir William James, commented on the 'good seamanship instruction, with boats, derricks, chains, etc. on the parade'.[9] During the war, *Collingwood* was bombed several times, with 30 ratings being killed by one attack in 1943.

In 1940, wireless telegraphy training was transferred from HMS *Vincent* and a Radio Direction Finding School added two years later. In 1946, *Collingwood* became a training establishment for officers and ratings in the maintenance of all electrical and radio equipment in the Fleet (except the Fleet Air Arm). Responsibility for weapons was added and, after several reorganisations and name changes, it became the Royal Navy's School of Communications and Weapon Engineering. It is now one of the largest training establishments in Europe, running over 1,000 courses with 6,000 students passing through each year.

Vosper

Though a private company, Vosper's contribution to the war effort merits its inclusion here. During the Second World War, over 300 Motor Torpedo Boats were made to Vosper's designs for the Allied navies, including 85 at Portsmouth and Portchester, and a further six by Camper and Nicholson at Gosport and Northam. An improved two-bladed propeller design, tested at the Admiralty Experimental Works, greatly improved the speed of Vosper's wartime craft. The company was started by Herbert Vosper, an engineer who, at the age of 21, established workshops on the Camber for the refitting and repairing of sea craft, including War Office and Admiralty launches. Vosper also designed, developed and built pioneering oil and semi-diesel engines, boilers, pumps and anchors. After a rapid expansion of its shipbuilding activities during the First World War, Herbert Vosper retired, and it was not until the early 1930s that the company began to concentrate on the development of fast craft. Increasing demand from the Admiralty led to the addition of a second shipyard at Flathouse Yard, and a third, in 1939, at Portchester. After the war, Vosper pioneered the development of diesel and gas turbines. In 1966 the company merged with John I. Thorneycroft & Co. Ltd. of Southampton and was successful in marketing vessels to foreign navies. In October 2000, Vosper Thorneycroft announced that its Woolston yard would close and that it planned to revive shipbuilding at Portsmouth Dockyard, though at the time of writing these plans remain unconfirmed.[10]

Chapter 13

OFF DUTY

207
The first Sailors' Home in Queen Street.

When a ship was in its home port the dangers of impressed men deserting persuaded most captains to confine their crews to the ship, an unpopular policy which was one of the complaints of men who took part in the Spithead and Nore mutinies of 1797.

Captains were not, however, entirely impervious to the needs and desires of their men and many turned a blind eye to the flotilla of boats full of prostitutes, or 'Solent Nymphs', which met every ship as it anchored at Spithead. The scenes that followed were likened to the biblical 'opening of the bottomless pit' in a campaigning pamphlet published by the Reverend G.C. Smith in Portsea in 1828.[1] Another pamphlet, by an outraged admiral, went into more detail:

> The men … go into the boats and pick out a woman (as one would choose cattle), paying a shilling or two to the boatman for her passage off … The whole of the shocking disgraceful transactions of the lower deck it is impossible to describe – the dirt, filth and stench; the disgusting conversation; the indecent, beastly conduct and horrible scenes; the blasphemy and swearing; the riots, quarrels, and fighting which often takes place, where hundreds of men and women are huddled together in one room, as it were, and where, in bed (each man being allowed only fourteen inches breadth for his hammock), they are squeezed between the next hammocks and must be witness of each other's actions … Let those who have never seen a ship of war picture to themselves a vary large low room (hardly capable of holding the men) with 500 men and probably 300 or 400 women of the vilest description shut up in it, and giving way to every excess of debauchery that the grossest passions of human nature can lead them to …[2]

The crews of ships who were not in their home port were normally permitted shore leave, and, because of the practice of withholding pay during long commissions, had a relatively large sum of money to dispose of in town. At the end of the 18th century there were 170 public houses in Portsmouth and 70 in Gosport, and contemporary estimates of the number of working prostitutes in the Portsmouth area ranged from 2,000 to 20,000, many of whom carried out their trade openly on the street, much to the shock of visitors.

In contemporary accounts the sailor and soldier were seen to be in need of protection from these hordes of prostitutes and,

indeed, from themselves. During the second half of the 19th century several individuals resolved to do what they could to help. The first Royal Sailors' Home was opened in 1852 in Queen Street, Portsea, and aimed to provide 'a comfortable, clean, respectable boarding or club-house to go to without fear of being robbed or exposed to temptation'. It had 24 beds and was ideally situated in one of the most notorious areas, but the strict regime made it unpopular. A similar institution, but without beds, the 'Sailors' Resort', was established in Gosport in 1869 by Henry Cook, an ex-Navy man who was concerned about the 'spiritually destitute condition' of seamen and fishermen.[3] Sailors, both merchant and navy, had access to a café and Christian reading room. Henry Cook also set up the Bethel Mission, and delivered bundles of tracts to ships at Spithead using a converted ferry boat manned by a crew of homeless boys from the Ragged School he had also founded.

In 1856 the Reverend Carus Wilson of Ventnor set up a Soldiers' Home on the corner of King Street and Lombard Street in Old Portsmouth to provide educational and recreational facilities for 5,000 men of the garrison. Carus Wilson had been concerned about the immoral temptations available in Newport to

the soldiers of Albany Barracks, but the situation in Portsmouth was far worse.[4]

The Home was short-lived, closing after Carus-Wilson died in 1859, but the need for such facilities began to be accepted. A report in 1861 alerted the War Department to the 'temptations leading to intoxication and lust that are very great at Portsmouth'. It alleged that 'within a circle having a radius of 1100 ft there are more than 100 public houses, many of which are known to be brothels in disguise'.[5]

After Carus-Wilson's death there was an understanding that the government would open similar facilities on a larger scale. But nothing materialised, and the idea was developed by Sarah Robinson, a Christian lady who, in spite of an incurable spine disease, devoted her life to the comfort and care of soldiers. With her support, a Marines' reading room was set up in Upper South Street in Gosport in around 1865, though this was relocated to Gosport High Street in 1866 and renamed the 'Royal Marines', Soldiers' and Sailors' Institute'.[6] Henry Cook also opened a Soldiers' Mission Room in Stoke Road, in addition to his Sailors' Resort.

Turning her attentions to Portsmouth, Sarah Robinson converted a notorious High Street pub, the *Fountain Inn*, into a Soldiers' Institute in 1874, providing men with somewhere to stay away from the temptations and dangers of prostitutes and 'land sharks', conmen who specialised in relieving seamen of their earnings. Sailors, marines and soldiers were all welcomed here. Troopships arriving or departing from harbour were visited and religious books and 'warming but not inebriating' coffee distributed by Miss Robinson and her staff, who also cared for soldiers' and sailors' widows and orphans. In 1879, the Sailors' Welcome, with 220 beds, was opened by Miss Robinson near the Dockyard gates, reflecting the increasing demand. These initiatives were funded by charitable donations from rich patrons, including Florence Nightingale, General Gordon and the Earl of Shaftesbury. Miss Robinson continued fundraising and carrying out similar work until the age of 81, when she transferred the Soldiers' Institute to the YMCA. This was during the First World War, when an average of 1,200 men used the facilities daily.

In the late 1870s, another benevolent Christian lady, Miss Aggie Weston, took over an old music hall in Commercial Road and converted it into a cafe and reading room; the idea, again, was to provide an alternative to the public house. Aggie Weston had already established a successful Sailors' Rest at Devonport with her partner Sophia Wintz, and had also promoted temperance groups on ships. The café was a great success, and in 1881 a new Sailors' Rest was built on donated land in Commercial Road. The building had 20 beds, but with the acquisition of adjoining sites over a number of years this expanded to 600. 'Aggie's', as it became known, flourished. Having turned his back on sex and alcohol, the 'new blue-jacket' appreciated good, inexpensive food, a hot bath, central heating, electric lighting, reading rooms, community singing, a quiet smoke, a game of billiards or chess and a mug of cocoa.[7] Initially, both Aggie Weston and Sarah Robinson encountered vociferous opposition

208 *(left)*
Debauchery at Portsmouth Point, *c*.1800 (details from an engraving based on Rowlandson's sketch).

209 *(below left)*
Royal Sailors' Rest in Commercial Road, *c*.1899.

210 *(below)*
Agnes Weston, founder of the Royal Sailors' Rest.

211
Interior of Royal Sailors' Rest, *c.*1899.

212
Sketches at the Royal Sailors' Rest, 1890.

to their initiatives. Even Queen Victoria is said to have doubted the wisdom of encouraging unmarried women to carry out such work. Local opposition came from the opposite end of the social scale, with stories of local prostitutes pelting both ladies with stones and mud. They are reported to have 'snarled and cursed' at Miss Robinson, accusing her of 'taking the bread out of other people's mouths'.[8] An effigy of her was ceremoniously burnt on Southsea Common.

Official concern about prostitution and the incidence of venereal disease in the Army and Navy resulted in the passing of the Contagious Diseases Act in 1864, which introduced powers enabling the police in some garrison towns to collect evidence for magistrates to hospitalise or imprison suspected infected prostitutes. Despite the harsh and brutal treatment this sanctioned, the act appears to have gone some way in controlling prostitution, with a 25 per cent fall in the number of known brothels in Portsmouth by 1870, and an 18 per cent reduction in the number of soldiers and sailors reporting sick in 1868-9.[9]

In 1904 the Trafalgar Services Club (later the Trafalgar Institute) was established in a Gothic-fronted building in Edinburgh Road. Five years later, the Duchess of Albany opened a Sailors' and Soldiers' Home a few yards up the road, though this was later to serve as Aggie Weston's Royal Sailors' Rest after the original buildings were bombed during the Second World War.

The aim of 'The Traf' was to provide comfortable lodgings, recreational facilities and good food for servicemen who were members of the Church of England. During the First World War soldiers of the British Expeditionary Force spent their last nights there before being sent to the trenches. Survivors later used it as a convalescent home.[10]

Following the Battle of Jutland in 1916, the lockers of nearly a hundred sailors and marines were cleared and their possessions forwarded to their next of kin.

SKETCHES AT THE SAILOR'S REST. PORTSMOUTH

IN THE SMOKING ROOM

SCRAMBLING FOR THE SIXPENCES FOR TEAS

AT THE COFFEE BAR

CROWDED OUT

A SKETCH IN THE READING ROOM 10 A.M.

SEPPINGS WRIGHT.

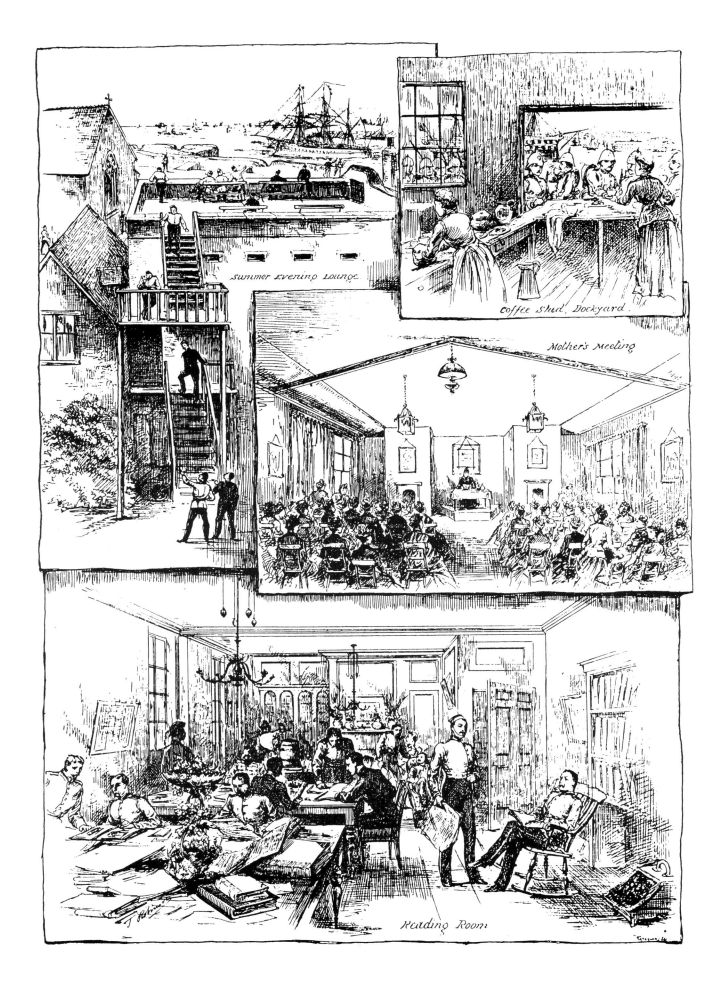

Summer Evening Lounge.

Coffee Shed, Dockyard.

Mother's Meeting

Reading Room

Unlike the former Soldiers' Institute, which was also destroyed in the war, the Traf survived incendiary bombing with the heroic help of some of the ratings who were staying there. By the end of the 1950s, nearly 4 million overnight stays had been recorded since its opening,[11] but with the running down of the Navy the club was closed in 1975 and converted into student accommodation.

During Portsmouth Football Club's post-war heyday, sailors would queue along the pavements after the match for sausage, egg and chips from the Traf restaurant. Pompey's terraces had always attracted off-duty sailors *en masse*, and many of its best players have been drawn from local service establishments.

213 *(left)*
Sketches at Sarah Robinson's Soldiers' Institute, 1889. (Also showing a Mothers' Meeting at Eastney and the distribution of coffee to troops at Portsmouth Dockyard.)

214 *(above)*
Popular images of 'Jack' from a postcard dated 1916 and as depicted in *Punch*, 1897.

215 *(top right)*
Trafalgar Institute entrance in Edinburgh Road.

216 *(bottom right)*
Royal Sailors' Home Club in Queen Street, as depicted on a post-war postcard.

217 *(left)*
Duchess of Albany's Sailors' and Soldiers' Home in Edinburgh Road.

218 *(above)*
Courtyard at Sailors' Home, Queen Street, 1887.

219 *(above right)*
Royal Marines in the Canteen garden, Eastney Barracks. This postcard is captioned on the reverse, 'Champion Heavy Weight Beer Shifters, 1919'.

220 *(far right)*
Sailors at the *Jubilee Arms* in St James Street (off Queen Street), Portsea.

221 *(right)*
A rare view of stokers outside a Portsmouth pub.

Indeed, the roots of the club are military, having drawn upon a successful Royal Artillery team which was thrown out of the English Amateur Cup in 1899 for breaching strict rules relating to amateurism.

The importance of having a fit and healthy Army and Navy, as well as a recognition of the individual character and team-spirit forming qualities of sport, resulted in the active promotion and integration of physical training and sport into the general training of servicemen. In the Navy this occurred after the abolition of sail, when men began to work for long periods with machinery in cramped conditions below deck. In 1888 a gymnastic training course was started at HMS *Excellent*, after which recruits were passed to the Army Gymnastic School at Aldershot.

In 1903 the Royal Naval Barracks was opened, providing luxuries that had been unheard of in the hulks that seamen were used to, including well-equipped games and recreation rooms and a gymnasium. In 1910 a purpose-built School of

222 (top)
About half the spectators are servicemen in this section of the crowd at a Pompey match in 1913.

223 (above)
Naval Police patrol leaving the Dockyard c.1899. These were notoriously hard men whose duty was described by the *Navy and Army Illustrated* as ensuring that 'Jack ashore on his Saturday to Monday leave is enjoying himself wisely and well'.

"LET ME LIKE A SOLDIER FALL."

226 *(inset below)*
Tattooist Albert Silmore at work in
Portsmouth between the wars.

227 *(bottom)*
HMS *Vernon* Cycling Club members,
*c.*1899.

224 *(left)*
Inter-service rivalry depicted on an
Edwardian postcard.

225 *(top)*
Billiard Room at RN Barracks,
*c.*1910.

Physical Training was opened in Pitt Street. The curriculum included boxing,
wrestling, swimming, fencing, judo and gymnastics, and, by 1920, team sports. It
remained at Pitt Street until 1988, when, as part of HMS *Temeraire*, it moved to
Burnaby Road. *Temeraire* was commissioned in 1971 and has developed into one
of the best equipped sports centres in the south, with a floodlit soccer pitch, swimming pool, indoor tennis courts, squash courts, fitness studio and gymnasium.[12]
   The United Services Ground was constructed by convict labour in the late
1870s on land that had become available after the demolition of redundant

228
Warrant Officers' Mess Annual
Dance, 1913.

229
Christmas in the Sergeants' Mess,
Forton Barracks, 1912.

ramparts and moats. Work also involved the filling in of the Mill Pond which had become 'exceedingly malodorous',[13] and the erection of a pavilion and grounds-man's cottage. The ground was initially run by the army and restricted to commissioned officers for many years, though other ranks were permitted by invitation or when they were needed to man the cricket scoring board.[14] After the Second World War, the ground passed to the Royal Navy and the facilities became available to all ranks. The Nuffield United Services Officers' Club, situated in the south-east corner of the ground, was opened in 1951 for officers and their families, but is now part of the University of Portsmouth.[15] Another club for commissioned naval and marine officers, the Royal Naval Club, was formed in 1867 and extended its premises in Pembroke Road several times to meet demand. It amalgamated with the exclusive Royal Albert Yacht Club in 1971.

Chapter 14

Naval and Military Hospitals

230
Patient being transferred to Haslar Hospital, 1897.

Before the opening of Haslar Hospital in 1753, thousands of wounded and sick seamen in the Portsmouth area were left at the mercy of unqualified and unscrupulous private contractors who received a shilling a head per day to look after them in 'sick lodgings', which were almost invariably ale-houses and hovels. This was not without its dangers for local residents. In 1628 the Mayor of Portsmouth wrote to the secretary of the Navy to complain that sick sailors who had returned from overseas brought with them diseases which had spread to the local population, with often fatal results.

A privately run hospital in Gosport was opened in 1713 and contracted by the Admiralty Board to help provide a more professional service. This hospital comprised a number of wooden sheds cheaply erected on a marshy area (in what is now Lees Lane). Up to 700 patients were crammed in, each extra head making additional profit. Every expense was spared in its operation and staffing, the wages being such that only second-rate medical staff worked there. The contractor, Nathaniel Jackson, named it Fortune Hospital, reflecting his own financial condition rather than the prognosis for those admitted to his care. An inquiry in 1744 blamed this private provision for many abuses, desertions and preventable deaths, and recommended the building of a Naval Hospital, though a similar recommendation made in 1653 had come to nothing. A cheap option to convert Portchester Castle into the new hospital was considered, but rejected as impracticable.

Work began on a 95 acre farm site overlooking the mouth of Portsmouth Harbour in 1746, and was eventually finished in 1762. The design of the massive main structure, comprising three blocks around an open courtyard, ensured that wards had all round lighting and ventilation. Most patients were brought in from their ships by boat to a jetty in Blockhouse Lake and pushed into the hospital in hand-carts, though this was later replaced by a rail system. By the end of the 18th century, between 1,500 and 2,000 patients were being treated in 84 wards at any one time.

Many patients had been 'pressed' into the navy against their will, and so escapes from Haslar were common, despite its isolated location. High iron railings were installed across the open end of the recreation area created by the three blocks to prevent this, though staff were often bribed to aid deserters, as well as to smuggle in alcohol. The sewerage system offered a favourite conduit for this traffic until a guard was stationed at the outlet. The high boundary walls were built as a further deterrent.

Accommodation for administrative officers and surgeons, a laundry and dispensary were also built, along with St Luke's Church where there is a memorial to the 'Father of Nautical Medicine', Dr. James Lind. Dr. Lind was Physician at Haslar from 1758 to 1783, and is best known for his advocacy of lemon juice as a cure for scurvy, but his research on preventing typhus also helped save many lives. Up until the end of the 19th century a large proportion of the hundreds of thousands of seamen treated at Haslar suffered from these diseases and syphilis. Relatively few required treatment or surgery as a result of war wounds as the time taken to return to port tended to kill or cure. A charge of fifteen shillings for the treatment of venereal disease was abolished in 1795, largely due to the lobbying of Dr. Thomas Trotter, a leading physician at Haslar. This resulted in more seamen volunteering for treatment, and at an earlier stage of the disease.[1] Soldiers suffering from venereal diseases were isolated and treated at Southsea Castle during the Napoleonic Wars.

One of Haslar's sea-facing wings was set aside as a 'lunatic asylum' for seamen who had been driven mad by the hardships and horrors of naval life and warfare. Dr. Trotter believed that impressment alone was a factor in bringing on mental illness, and recorded that some men actually died as a result of this legal kidnapping.[2] In 1838 there were 118 mental patients being looked after at Haslar. They were routinely subjected to severe discipline and brutal treatment which, it was believed, was in their interests. Bleeding, blistering and other tortures were used to purge men of their illnesses. Physical abuse, restraint with straitjackets and solitary confinement continued into the 20th century. A strip of land that led down to the sea, known as the 'lunatics' airing grounds', was a place where men could take refuge. In 1910 a new 'mental department' was built on the sea wall and was in use until the early 1960s when patients were transferred to the Joint Services Hospital at Netley.

The mental department was one of a number of additional buildings added between the 1880s and the end of the First World War. These included the landmark red-brick Water Tower (1885), the Pathology Laboratory (1899), Medical and Sisters' Messes (1901), Zymotic Hospital (1902) and the Sick Officers' Block (1905). To cope with the influx of casualties in the First World War, temporary facilities were established at the Brodrick Hall in Clayhall Road, Whale Island and Flathouse Road.[3]

The training of medical officers began at Haslar in 1880, sowing the seed of what became the Royal Naval Medical School (established in Greenwich in 1912) which moved to its present site at Monckton House, Alverstoke in 1948. With better general health and medical advances, priorities shifted into research into

231 *(top left)*
Haslar Hospital, *c.*1850.

232
Haslar Main Block and North Wing, *c.*1897.

233
Senior Medical Officers' residences, *c.*1897.

234
Haslar Main Block from the Quadrangle, *c.*1897.

235 *(above)*
Royal Naval Medical School, Monckton House, 1966.

236 *(top left)*
Haslar entrance, *c.*1897.

237 *(above)*
Convalescents in the 'Airing Grounds' which was situated between the South Wing and the sea.

238 *(left)*
Nurses at Haslar, *c.*1897. In the centre is the Head Sister, Miss Louisa Hogg.

239 *(below left)*
A less formal portrait of nurses at Haslar, celebrating a royal occasion, believed to have been taken in the mid-1930s.

240 *(right)*
Scenes at Haslar, *c.*1897, from top: the dispensary; the kitchen; the steam laundry; mending clothes.

the physiology of survival at sea, motion sickness, underwater medicine and the effects of radiation in the event of a reactor or weapon accident. The Defence Radiological Protection Service was established here to provide advice and training to the armed services. In 1969 the school was renamed the Institute of Naval Medicine.

Haslar survived the Second World War relatively unscathed, though the Library, Museum and some of the residences were destroyed in air raids. The hospital cellars were used as shelters for staff and patients. Over 3,000 sick berth attendants were trained here in the war years, and 83,446 patients treated (including James Callaghan, the Portsmouth-born, future Prime Minister).[4] Local people contributed to a blood bank, set up to cope with casualties from the Normandy landings. The hospital also played a vital role in the supply of medical stores and equipment to ships.

Haslar has treated the sick and wounded from every major conflict from the Napoleonic Wars to the Falklands War. Since World War Two and the setting up of the National Health Service, civilians have been admitted in increasing numbers until, in recent years, Haslar has fulfilled the role of a District General Hospital for the Gosport area, at the same time as providing a service to 37,000 service personnel. In 1998 the Government revealed plans to close Haslar, though this was met with fierce resistance by the local community. In 2000, an 'Accident Treatment Centre' was in operation, staffed entirely by nursing staff rather than doctors.

Though Haslar also treated sick marines, a hospital specifically for marines was in existence in Spring Street in Portsmouth in the 1820s. This appears to have reopened as the Royal Marine Infirmary in the Gunwharf, serving the Royal Marine Artillery, which was resident there in the period 1824-58.[5]

The first military hospital in Portsmouth was built in 1680 on the site of a monastery near the Old Gunwharf. By 1694 it had been converted into accommodation for soldiers, surviving into the 20th century as Colewort Barracks. Another was built in Lion Terrace, a small and bleak wooden building where the sick and wounded of the Napoleonic War period were treated. The building was demolished shortly after the Battle of Waterloo, and, in 1833, another built on a battery in the Inner Camber with an entrance from White Hart Row. In 1853-4, a new Military Hospital (also known as Station Hospital) was built on the same site in Lion Terrace. This was described as 'handsome and commodious', measuring 120 yards in length and divided into large and small apartments where up to 300 wounded soldiers of the Crimean War were treated at any one time.

241 *(top left)*
Entrance to the Alexandra Royal
Military Hospital (now Queen
Alexandra), *c.*1915.

242 *(bottom left)*
Arrival of wounded men at Fawcett
Road hospital during the First World
War.

243 *(above and right)*
Wounded soldiers convalescing at
Portsmouth and on South Parade Pier
during the First World War.

In 1898 the Military Hospital and the nearby Anglesea Barracks were transferred to the Admiralty, who arranged for a replacement hospital to be built on the
former Wymering Farm Estate on the slopes of Portsdown Hill. The Alexandra
Royal Military Hospital was opened in 1908 to serve the men of the Portsmouth
Garrison and surrounding area as far as Dorchester and Winchester. There were
four wards for officers, eight for men, and a separate mental ward with a padded
room.

The 220 beds were more than doubled during the First World War, when huts
were erected in the grounds. Temporary military hospitals and convalescent
wards were also set up at Milton Infirmary (St Mary's), the Eye and Ear Hospital,
the Girls' Secondary School in Fawcett Road, Brankesmere in Queen's Crescent,
Oatlands in Kingston Crescent, Brookfield House and the National Children's
Home in Alverstoke. Men who had been driven mad in the trenches, or at sea, and

were unfit to remain in the services, were consigned to the Lunatic Asylum in Locksway Road (later St James's Hospital). These poor, haunted men were a familiar sight in the Milton neighbourhood for many years.[6]

After the war, what became known as Queen Alexandra Hospital (Q.A.) was used for the care of disabled veterans, but during the Second World War the first civilian casualties were admitted. Following D-Day, further blocks and extensions were added to cope with the wounded, but after the setting up of the National Health Service, the hospital's military role declined as it gradually became a general hospital. In 1953 the Portsmouth branch of the British Limbless Ex-Servicemen's Association (BLESMA) raised enough money to open a home on the corner of Eastern Parade and Bruce Road for the care of severely disabled veterans.

The public cemeteries of the area contain many naval and military memorials, graves and war graves. Southsea promenade and Victoria Park play host to several monuments and memorials that are reminders of Britain's imperial past. However, some memorials to those who died in defence of their country have not survived. The War Memorial Gateway at the Royal Hospital, was demolished in 1969, while graves at Mile End Cemetery were lost in the expansion of the Continental Ferryport. Proposals to level Highland Cemetery, which contains war graves (including those of seven men who were awarded the Victoria Cross), were withdrawn after public protest in the early 1990s.

Irreverence is not, however, a modern phenomenon. With the opening of Haslar in 1753, unconsecrated burial grounds were set aside in the south-west corner of the site for those who succumbed to their illnesses and wounds. Like those who died at sea, their graves went unmarked. Dr. Lind recorded 1,716 hospital deaths alone in 1779-80. Thousands of men who died of typhus after fighting in the Peninsular War are buried here, as are the 600 victims of the *Royal George*, which capsized in 1782. On the shores of Forton Creek, over 1,000 French sailors and soldiers, killed by grim prison conditions, were buried without respect or ceremony in two makeshift cemeteries.

By the 1820s, deaths at Haslar were properly recorded and interments were made in a part of the burial grounds that had been walled off and consecrated. But with the ground being full, literally, to overflowing with human remains a new cemetery was needed, and in 1859 an area by Stoke Lake in Clayhall was consecrated and a chapel built. It appears that some bodies were disinterred and reburied at the new cemetery.

Deaths of men at sea were quickly followed by individual burials at sea, the body being carefully sewn into a hammock,

244 (*left*)
Portsmouth War Memorial unveiling ceremony, 19 October 1921.

245 (*bottom left*)
Sentimental Victorian tableau depicting a sailor's grave.

246 (*below*)
Naval funeral at Haslar Cemetery, *c*.1907.

247 (*bottom right*)
Battle of Jutland Memorial Service in Victoria Park, 1916.

248 (*right*)
The Naval War Memorial was unveiled in 1924 and commemorates the 9,666 Portsmouth-based sailors who died in the First World War and, as the inscription reads, 'have no other grave but the sea'. An extension commemorating the 14,797 sailors and marines that died in the Second World War was unveiled in 1953.

weighted, draped in a Union Jack and slipped into the deep. Three volleys were fired over the spot by the dead man's shipmates who bid for his possessions, giving more than their worth because proceeds were sent to the departed's widow or parents.

The same funeral ceremonials were carried out at Haslar, conducted by the chaplain of the ship who waited at the cemetery gates for the flag-draped coffin to arrive, preceded by the firing party. The mourners, juniors and officers in charge, with cocked hats, epaulettes and swords, followed. As an observer wrote in 1901,

> Born in most instances, in a humble sphere of life, and forming during his life a very small unit in a crowd (the sailor) is taken to his last resting place with considerable pomp and circumstance far in excess of what would be considered due in civil life; for the humblest individual in His Majesty's forces is held to be entitles to military honours at his funeral, and no one surely would begrudge him this distinction.[7]

But there was to be no such distinction in war when the scale of local casualties made such ceremonials impracticable. Hundreds of local sailors and marines died in the space of a week in the Battle of Jutland and the sinking of HMS *Hampshire* in 1916. This was a turning point for many who had been brought up to believe in the invincibility of the British Navy. The Jutland memorial service, which packed Victoria Park, was a mass public demonstration of mourning, at the same time as showing the 'pomp, circumstance and honour' that was denied those who had been killed. Impressive stone memorials served the same purpose. The Navy War Memorial on Southsea Common commemorates the thousands of local men who were killed in the two world wars and 'have no other grave but the sea'. The civic war memorial in the Guildhall Square was unveiled in 1921, and that practical legacy, the War Memorial Hospital in Gosport, was opened in 1923, both having been built with public donations.

249
Memorial card for a Gosport marine, 1922.

Chapter 15

FLEET REVIEWS AND MILITARY DISPLAYS

Firing a feu de joie.

250
A *feu de joie* on Southsea Common during the Coronation Review of 1902.

The origins of the Royal Fleet Review as a formal and celebrated occasion date back to 1773 when George III set out from Kew in the Royal Coach to be greeted by a 'triple discharge of cannon', and escorted in the Royal Barge to Spithead by admirals and captains, resplendent in gold-braided tricorne hats, wigs, lace-edged waistcoats, white silk stockings and silver-buckled shoes. The King inspected the veterans of the Seven Years War, who were soon to fight the French again in the War of American Independence. This is considered to be the first official Review by the Admiralty, though there were many previous occasions when inspections were made by monarchs, prior to embarking on foreign expeditions. Early examples are Edward III, who reviewed his fleet of 1,600 ships, and Henry V, who reviewed 1,400 ships before setting sail for France.[1]

Queen Victoria conducted a 'Grand Naval Review' in 1853, and a 'Grand Peace Review' after the Crimean War, in 1856. The latter was reported to have attracted 600,000 spectators to the area, including excursions from France and Germany, and was widely reported in the international press. By this time the importance of such displays of strength as a deterrent to potential enemies, as well as a reassurance to the British public, was not lost on the government. The Solent, according to one observer, 'groaned under the number and variety of craft'.[2] Impressive and romantic, three-decker 'wooden walls', 'with twelve hundred souls on board', were viewed alongside new innovations, such as 'screw-propelled ships' and boats 'encased in armour'. Over one hundred gunboats took part, 'puffing away like locomotive engines with wisps of white steam training from their funnels'. Many people in the Portsmouth area, taking advantage of the huge influx of visitors, rented out rooms and were able to charge an average of three or four guineas for one night (a sum that was over two months pay for an Ordinary Seaman). One reporter was unhappy at having to spend the night in 'a stiff-backed chair in a kitchen', while another slept on a billiard table. They were not the only ones to suffer. Children and babies were reported to have lost their beds, cots and cradles to 'London ladies', though it was not known where they had been put. Two hundred

policemen were brought in from London to help the local force in the event of trouble, though it seems that they were not needed as they were seen drinking beer, flirting with girls and joining in the celebrations.[3]

Fleet Reviews were not only profitable to householders with rooms to let. With tens of thousands of bluejackets in port, as well as those from foreign navies, publicans and prostitutes also did a roaring trade, with women travelling from London, Aldershot and Southampton to solicit a share in the business.

In Queen Victoria's reign, Fleet Reviews became a feature of royal anniversaries and visits by foreign monarchs. Queen Victoria's Diamond Jubilee Review in 1897 boasted the greatest assembly of warships ever gathered at anchorage. The hardware on show – formidable iron-clads cluttered with barbettes and bristling with turret guns – demonstrated to the world that the Empire was invincible and its will could be imposed. *Jane's Fighting Ships*, published for the first time in this year, confirmed that the Queen's Empire had 53 ironclads and armoured cruisers, 21 more than the nearest rival, France. The foreign press and heads of state, together with patriotic crowds who lined Southsea Beach, Stokes Bay and the shores of the Isle of Wight, were awed by the spectacle:

> We showed that our sovereignty over the sea is far reaching and absolute … In all about 165 ships of our Navy rode at ease in four long lines and two short ones in the narrow strait, and they were manned by 40,000 officers and men. The length of the lines of British ships aggregated nearly thirty miles! … Power is still sweet to the ruling race; that the Empire which has been bought with the blood of the Anglo-Saxon will be maintained in its integrity at any cost. Here they lay in serried ranks on the moving waters, orderly as soldiers on a parade ground – the steel-clad champions of a nation's honour – as powerful to compel peace as to

251 *(far left)*
Spectators at Fort Monckton during the Naval Review of 1856.

252 *(left)*
Coronation Review souvenir, 1953, and *News* Silver Jubilee Fleet Review souvenir, 1977.

253 *(above)*
Depiction of Victoria's Diamond Jubilee Review of 1897.

254 *(below)*
Cruisers leaving Spithead after a Naval Display, 1912.

put the issue of war out of the question if war must come. [The Review] provided a sublime spectacle for our Colonial and foreign visitors, and it taught a lesson that was meant to be learned by the whole World, and was actually so learned. A great military Power we might not be, but on the seas our dominion was, and must ever be, unquestionable.[4]

A sudden thunderstorm, however, pricked the patriotic moment, drenched the spectators, and the mighty fleet was lost in an impenetrable haze. Within a few years the ships in the mist had been superseded, rendered obsolete by advances in ship design, armour and weaponry. All Fleet Reviews demonstrated the latest innovations. In 1897 the first turbine-propelled ship, the *Turbinia*, was featured, while the increased frequency of reviews carried out by Edward VII reflected the developments arising from the escalating arms race with Germany, triggered by the launch of the *Dreadnought* in 1906. The 1911 Review boasted the state-of-the-art Super-Dreadnought, *Neptune*. The 1914 Review introduced aircraft for the first time. This Review was followed by a test mobilisation involving 24 Dreadnoughts, 35 battleships, 49 cruisers, 76 submarines and 78 destroyers, manned by nearly 100,000 sailors. Three weeks later, war was declared.

Fleet Reviews were often complemented by shows of military strength by the local garrison, successive Commanders of which were keen to avoid being sidelined completely by the 'senior service'. During the 1914 Review the Commander of the Garrison positioned his men along the shore from South Parade Pier to Point and from Haslar Hospital to Gilkicker. On hearing the Fleet make its Royal Salute, the three-mile line of soldiers fired their rifles, consecutively, into the air.

The *feu de joie* was a feature of royal occasions. In 1801, a grand review of 6,000 regulars, militia and volunteers took place on Portsdown Hill in honour of the King's birthday. After giving a general salute, the artillery fired three rounds in turn and there followed a *feu de joie* and three cheers for the King. During the latter half of the 19th century, large scale military exercises were regularly conducted in the Portsdown and Hilsea area to help test defences and train volunteers in something akin to battle conditions. This aim, however, was hindered by the large number of spectators who turned up to view the spectacle, which was often held at Easter weekend.[5] It was a tradition to 'go up the Hill' and enjoy the view or the fair. The drama and colour offered by a mock-battle was irresistible, and it was free.

Volunteers came from all over the south, including London, to take part in these manoeuvres, many of whom detrained at Petersfield to act as an army attacking Portsmouth from the north. The national press gave considerable coverage to the spectacle, with enterprising reporters employing observation balloons:

> The army of defenders as it arrived from Portsmouth took up its position on Portsdown Hill, and was powerfully supported by the Naval Flotilla of gunboats moored in Portchester Lake. Perhaps the most exciting part of the whole fight was when the enemy was driven back into Cosham and a regular hand-to-hand fight ensued with the defenders, every foot of ground being hotly contended for. The excitement was contagious; for the villagers and others who mixed with the troops appeared to be as much interested as the volunteer combatants themselves, while women and children, some frightened, others pleased, and all greatly astonished, looked out from their doors and windows...After two hours hard fighting the enemy effected a retreat over the Hill towards Fareham … Little need we fear the invasion of foreign enemies if 'England's gallant Defenders' will show the same amount of pluck under substantial fire as they did under the stifling smell of gunpowder, the suffocating dust, and the glaring sun of April 13th.[6]

The value of the Volunteer Manoeuvres, as with Fleet Reviews, appears to have had little to do with training, but rather to provide reassurance for the British public that the country was

255 *(below left)*
The Royal Yacht *Victoria and Albert* passing Clarence Pier, *c.*1911.

256 *(below)*
Navy Days, view of HMS *Victory* and submarines, *c.*1955.

257 *(right)*
Views of the Coronation Review of 1911 from the *Superb (top)* and from the *Lord Nelson.*

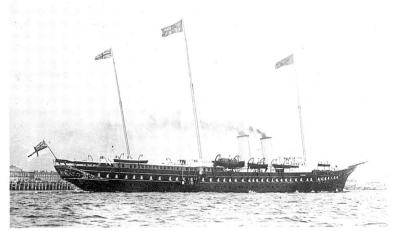

258 *(above left)*
Military Review on Southsea
Common, *c.*1905.

259 *(below)*
Spectators of Volunteer Manoeuvres,
1899. Visitors came from the
surrounding countryside and 'many a
youngster returns home fired with
military ardour, and yearning for a
time when he will don the red coat
and be the observed rather than the
observer'.

260 *(right)*
Volunteers on their way to
Portsmouth from Petersfield (1), the
Prince of Wales and his entourage
passing through the Triumphal Arch
at Cosham (2), flag signalling (3) and
the march-past of the London
Scottish (4), 1882.

invincible, and to serve as a warning to potential invaders that they would be seen off with little effort. On the ground, defences were adjusted and tactics honed, but the inability of a minority of the volunteers to take the sham-fight seriously, and the care that had to be taken to prevent men trespassing on private land (lest land-owners press compensation claims), combined with the hordes of spectators who accompanied the men on their raids, raises questions as to their practical use.

The sights and sounds of military bands, tattoos, parades and gun salutes were constant reminders of the presence of the garrison. The firing of the morning, midday and evening gun on the King's or the Duke of York's Bastions served a useful purpose at a time when the majority of the population could not afford a

timepiece. Much of this ceremonial activity centred on Grand Parade and the old ramparts, and the 'morning guard mounting' and evening tattoo were popular spectacles for all classes. The marking of the end of the day in Portsmouth by the garrison and the ships in Harbour is described by the Victorian novelists Walter Besant and James Rice in *By Celia's Arbour*:

> Then the evening gun from the Duke of York's bastion proclaimed the death of another day with a loud report, which made the branches in the trees above us to shake and tremble. And from the barracks in the town, from the Harbour Admiral's flagship, from the Port Admiral's flagship, from the flagship of the Admiral of the Mediterranean Fleet, then in harbour, from the tower of the old church, there came such a firing of muskets, such a beating of drums, playing of fifes, ringing of bells, and sounding of trumpets that you would have thought the sun was setting once for all, and receiving his farewell salute from a world he was leaving for ever …[7]

261 *(above)*
Portsmouth Garrison rifle meeting at Browndown, *c.*1875.

262 *(left)*
The midday gun on the King's Bastion, *c.*1882.

ABBREVIATIONS (SOURCES) AND NOTES

BPD	*Borough of Portsmouth Directory* (1859)
Gates 1900	Gates, W. G., *Illustrated History of Portsmouth* (1900)
Gates 1926	Gates, W. G., *Portsmouth in the Past* (1926)
GR	*The Graphic*
GOS	Gosport Records
HM	*Hampshire Magazine*
ILN	*Illustrated London News*
MM	*Mariner's Mirror*
NAI	*Navy and Army Illustrated*
NN	*Navy News*
NR	*Naval Review*
NRS	Naval Records Society
PN	*Portsmouth News*
PP	*The Portsmouth Papers*, published by Portsmouth City Council
PRC (1835-1927)	Gates, W. G. (ed.), *City of Portsmouth Records of the Corporation, 1835-1927* (1928)
PRC (1928-30)	Gates, W. G. (ed.), *City of Portsmouth Records of the Corporation, 1928-30* (1931)
PRC (1946-55)	Barnett, G.E. & Blanchard, V., *City of Portsmouth Records of the Corporation, 1946-55* (c. 1956)

Chapter 1: Fortifications
1. Gates (1900), p.111.
2. PRC (1928-30), pp.8-9.
3. Williams, G.H., 'The Western Defences of Portsmouth Harbour 1400-1800', *PP*, No. 30 (1979), pp.58-9.
4. Gates, *op. cit.*, p.597.
5. Gates (1926), p.42.
6. 'The Fortifications of Portsmouth', *Alverstoke Parish Magazine*, April 1864, p.3
7. *ILN*, 8 April 1882, p.339.
8. Jenkins, P., *Battle Over Portsmouth* (1986), pp.111-13

Chapter 2: The Army and Its Barracks
1. A list of Captain and Governors of Portsmouth appears in East, R., *Extracts from the Portsmouth Records* (1891), pp.635-40.
2. Gates (1900), p.218.
3. PRC (1928-30), p.xxxii.
4. Curling, H., *Recollections of Rifleman Harris* (1929), p.91.
5. Beloff, M., *Public Order and Popular Disturbances 1660-1714* (1938), p.112.
6. Gates, *op. cit.*, p.284.
7. Wilkins, R., *The Borough: being a faithful, tho' humorous description of one of the strongest garrisons and seaport towns in Great Britain* (1748), p.14.
8. East, *op. cit.*, pp.422-34.
9. Curling, *op. cit.*, pp.4-5.
10. Hoad, M.J., 'Porsmouth as others have seen it, Part I', *PP*, No. 15 (1972), p.16.
11. Marsh, A.J., 'When the Army fought the Navy', *Hampshire Magazine*, December 1977, p.64.
12. *Portsmouth Volunteer Training Corps Gazette*, May 1916, p.1.
13. *ILN*, 'Preparations for War', 4 March 1854.
14. Watson, C.M., *History of the Corps of Royal Engineers*, Vol. III (1914). This did not happen, of course.
15. Foster, A.E.M., 'The Unmaking of "Tommy"', *NAI*, 29 September 1900, p.42.
16. Dorril, S., *MI6: Inside the Covert World of Her Majesty's Secret Intelligence Service* (2000), pp.783-800, and Norton-Taylor, R., 'What's in that book?', *Guardian*, 24 January 2001.

Chapter 3: Sea Soldiers – The Royal Marines
1. PRC (1835-1927), p.299.
2. Jane, F., 'By sea and by land – the RMLI at Forton Barracks', *Good Words* (1897), pp.23-31.
3. 'Behind the Bars' (RM Band Service), *NN*, May 1999.

Chapter 4: The Dockyard
1. East, R., *Extracts from the Portsmouth Records* (1891), p.782.
2. *Ibid.*, p.782.
3. Hoad, M.J., 'Portsmouth as others have seen it, Part 1', *PP*, No. 15 (1972), p.18.
4. Allen, L., *The History of Portsmouth* (1817), p.162.
5. 'Portsmouth Dockyard', *BPD* (1859), p.256.
6. Riley, R., 'The evolution of the docks and the Industrial Buildings in Portsmouth Royal Dockyard 1698-1914', *PP*, No. 44 (1985), pp.22-5.
7. King, I.E., 'Forty Years of Change at Portsmouth Dockyard', *NR*, Vol. 43, 1955, pp.301-2.
8. 'Back to the Glory Days', *PN*, 13 October 2000.

Chapter 5: Victualling
1. Gates (1900), pp.112-13.
2. Mills, R., 'Country's oldest naval building lost for 150 years', *HM*, July 1963, pp.29-30.
3. 'Manufacture of ship-biscuit by machinery', *Saturday Magazine*, 29 April 1837, p.155.
4. Hoad, M.J. and Patterson, A.T., 'Portsmouth and the Crimean War', *PP*, No. 19, (1973), p.7.
5. 'Closure of Royal Clarence Yard', *First Base*, July 1995, p.38.
6. Parkes, O., 'Silver Jubilee 1910-1935', *ILN* (1935), p.44.
7. Sadden, J., *Keep the Home Fires Burning* (1990), pp.15-17.

Chapter 6: Feeding the Guns
1. Gates (1900), p.113.
2. *Ibid.*, p.384.
3. Slight, H., *Chronicles of Portsmouth* (1828), p.168.
4. *BPD*, p.257; *ILN*, 5 May 1855, pp.441-2; Allen, L. *The History of Portsmouth* (1817), pp.160-2.
5. 'About Priddy's Hard', *Hampshire Telegraph*, 5 May 1900.

Chapter 7: Naval Recruitment and Education
1. Saunders, W.H., *The Annals of Portsmouth* (1880).
2. Lloyd, C., *The British Seaman* (1970), p.171.
3. Religious Tract Society, *Sea Sketches about Ships and Sailors* (c.1880), p.96.
4. *PRC* (1928-30), p.cviii.
5. R. Pococke in Hoad, M., 'Portsmouth as others have seen it 1540-1790', *PP*, No. 15 (1972), p.18.
6. 'Nobly, nobly Gosport's St. Vincent died away', *PN*, 9 December 1968.
7. 'T.S. *Foudroyant*', *NR*, Vol. 38 (1950), p.229-30.

Chapter 8: Naval Gunnery Training
1. *NAI*, Vol. II, No. 14, 26 June 1896, p.10

Chapter 9: Underwater Warfare
1. 'Torpedo warfare demonstrations', *ILN*, 25 January 1879, pp.375-6.
2. 'Submarine Miners and their work', *NAI*, 22 January 1897, pp.80-2.
3. Turner, J.F., *Service Most Silent: The Navy's Fight Against Enemy Mines* (1955), pp.59-67.
4. Halden, R., 'Men who defuse bombs', *HM*, June 1995, p.27.
5. PRC (1835-1927, pp.218-19, p.248.
6. *War Illustrated*, 'B11's Exploit: The Most Daring of the War', 26 December 1914, p.443.
7. Warner W.E., *A Short History of Fort Blockhouse* (1947), p.29.
8. 'HMS *Dolphin* decommissioned', *PN*, 15 September 1998.

Chapter 10: Defence in the Air
1. *Portsmouth Times*, 17 May 1911.
2. 'Naval display at Spithead', *Sphere Supplement*, 13 July 1912.
3. Burton, I., *Gosport Goes to War* (1981), p.55.
4. 'Falklands veteran's new pride', *PN*, 3 November 1994.

Chapter 11: Naval Communication, Navigation and Radar
1. PRC (1835-1927), p.48, and Gates (1900), pp.491-2.
2. PRC (1928-30), pp.82-3.

Chapter 12: Naval Barracks and Other Establishments
1. Dannreuther, H.E., *R.N. Barracks, Portsmouth and its History* (1932), p.10.
2. *Hampshire Telegraph*, 3 October 1903.
3. The *Sphere*, 10 November 1906, p.118.
4. Lloyd, C., *The Birtish Seaman* (1970), pp.226-7.
5. 'Computer's role is service to the Fleet', *PN*, 17 October 1970; 'Big new Navy base grows at Rowner', *PN*, 20 November 1970.
6. Dannreuther, *op. cit.*, p.56.

7. 'Excellent by name', *First Base*, No. 2 (1995), pp.16-17.
8. 'Gosport welcomes HMS Sultan', *PN*, 31 May 1956.
9. James, William, *The Portsmouth Letters* (1946) .
10. 'Back to the Glory Days', *PN*, 13 October 2000.

Chapter 13: Off Duty
1. Smith, G.C., *The first part of a humble address to the Lord Bishop of London concerning the general admission of unmarried females into British ships of war* (1828), p.17.
2. Hawkins (Admiral), *Statement of certain immoral practices in HM Ships* (1822) (published anonymously).
3. Isaacs, A.P., 'A Gosport man of faith and the sea', *HM*, June 1969, pp.36-7.
4. Matthews, J., 'William Carus Wilson – the Soldiers' Friend', *HM*, February 1985, pp.53-4.
5. Jackson, P., *Reports relating to Soldiers' Institutes – Portsmouth* (1861).
6. Robinson, S., *A Life Record* (1898), pp.280-3.
7. 'The Royal Sailors' Rests', *NAI*, 28 January 1899, pp.450-3.
8. Robinson, S., *My Book* (1914), p.155.
9. Portsmouth Literary and Philosophical Society, *Press Cuttings* (1871-3).
10. Kennett, M., 'Goodbye to the "Traf"', *HM*, July 1975, pp.49-50.
11. Trafalgar Services Club, *Annual Report 1959* (c.1960).
12. 'Fighting Temeraire', *NN*, December 1993.
13. PCR (1835-1927), p.312.
14. Kennett, M., 'Where the Navy plays host to Hampshire cricket', *HM*, August 1968, pp.32-3.
15. PCR (1946-55), p.111.

Chapter 14: Naval and Military Hospitals
1. Lloyd, C., 'The health of seamen', *NRS*, Vol. CVII, 1965, pp.228-9.
2. Tate, W., *A History of Haslar* (1906), p.142.
3. Sadden, J., *Keep the Home Fires Burning – the story of Portsmouth and Gosport in World War 1* (1990), pp.65-8.
4. Clark, G., *Doc – 100 year history of the Sick Berth Branch* (1984), p.75; Callaghan, J., *Time and Chance* (1987), p.59.
5. PCR (1835-1927), p.299.
6. Sadden, *op. cit.*, pp.65-8.
7. 'The last honours to a seaman', *NAI*, 15 June 1901, p.297.

Chapter 15: Fleet Reviews and Military Displays
1. Gates (1900), pp.62-5.
2. Saunders, W.H., *The Annals of Portsmouth* (1880), p.194.
3. *ILN*, 10 May 1856, pp.493-4.
4. Steevens, G.W. in Maxwell, H., *Sixty Years a Queen* (1897), p.227.
5. Thorpe, F.H., 'The Battle of Portsdown Hill', *HM*, September 1968, p.27.
6. *The Times*, 13 April 1868.
7. Besant, W. and Rice, J., *By Celia's Arbour: a Tale of Portsmouth Town* (1892), p.9.

BIBLIOGRAPHY

Chapter 1: Fortifications

Corney, A., *Fortifications in Old Portsmouth* (1965)

Gates, W. (1900)

Gates, W. (1926)

Lloyd, David W., *Buildings of Portsmouth and its Environs* (1974)

Moore, D. et al, *Solent Papers*, Nos. 1-6

Patterson, B.H., *A Military Heritage: A History of Portsmouth & Portsea Town Fortifications* (1984)

Patterson, A. Temple, 'Palmerston's Folly – The Portsdown and Spithead Forts', *PP*, No. 3 (1968)

PRC (1835-1927)

Quail, S., Stone Towers in Webb, J., et al, *The Spirit of Portsmouth: A History* (1989)

Rigold, S.E., *Portchester Castle* (1965)

Saunders, A.D., 'Hampshire Coastal Defence since the introduction of Artillery', *Archaeological Journal*, Vol. CXXIII, May 1967

Williams, G.H., 'The Western Defences of Portsmouth Harbour 1400-1800', *PP*, No. 30 (1979)

Chapter 2: The Army and its Barracks

Geddes, A., 'Portsmouth During the Great French Wars 1770-1800', *PP*, No. 9 (1970)

Harfield, A., Story of the Gosport Barracks, *HM*, January 1986

Hoad, M.J., 'Portsmouth and the Crimean War', *PP*, No. 19 (1973)

Hoad, M.J., 'Portsmouth – as others have seen it, Part I', *PP*, No. 15 (1972)

Hoad, M.J., 'Portsmouth – as others have seen it, Part II', *PP*, No. 20 (1973)

Jordan, R., 'Portsmouth in the Glorious Revolution of 1688', *PP*, No. 54 (1988)

Milldam House (leaflet) (1993)

Rigold, S.E., *Portchester Castle* (1965)

Saunders, W., *Annals of Portsmouth* (1880)

Venables, D., *Forton Barracks, 1807-1923*, GOS, No. 12 (1976)

Webb, R., *St George Barracks, Gosport, and the Country About* (1972)

Williams, G. H., *The Keys of the Fortress*, GOS, No. 13 (1977)

Williams, G.H. and B.D., *Defence of Stokes Bay against the Spanish Armada Part III and IV*, GOS, Nos. 6 and 7 (1973)

Chapter 3: Sea Soldiers – The Royal Marines

Clark, G., *Britain's Naval Heritage* (1981)

'Excellent by name', *First Base*, No. 2 (1995)

Lane, A., *The Royal Marines Barracks, Eastney* (1998)

'Farewell Marines', *PN* (supplement) (1991)

PRC (1835-1927)

Venables, D., *Forton Barracks 1807-1923*, GOS, No. 12 (1976)

Chapter 4: The Dockyard

BPD (section on Portsmouth Dockyard) (1859)

Coad, J., Historic Architecture of HM Naval Base, Portsmouth 1700-1850, *MM*, Vol. 67, No. 1, February 1981

Gates, W. (1900)

Gates, W., *A Naval Chronology* (1931)

Hoad, M., 'Portsmouth – As others have seen it 1540-1790', *PP*, No. 15 (1972)

Rodger, N.A.M., *The Admiralty* (1979)

Chapter 5: Victualling

Burton, L., *Gosport goes to war* (1981)

Coad, J., 'Historic architecture of HM Naval Base, Portsmouth 1700-1850', *MM*, Vol. 67, No. 1, February 1981

Gates, W. (1900)

Hoad, M.J. and Patterson, A.T., 'Portsmouth and the Crimean War', *PP*, No. 19 (1973)

Huggett, F.E., *Life and work at sea* (1975)

Leyland, J., 'Victualling the Navy – The Royal Clarence Yard, Gosport', in *NAI* , 21 September 1901

Maben, D., 'Growing up with the hulk', *HM*, February 1993

Merritt, J., 'Naval victualling and the development of the Royal Clarence Victualling Yard (until 1870)' (unpublished)

Strange, K.H., 'Jonas Hanway of the 18th century', *HM*, February 1984.

Surrey, N.W. and Thomas, J.H., *Book of Original Entries, 1731-51*, Portsmouth Record Series (1976)

Taylor, J., *Jonas Hanway* (1985)

Thrower, W.R., *Life at Sea in the Age of Sail* (1972)

Webb, R., *St George Barracks, Gosport and the Country About* (1972)

Woodall, R.R., 'Portsea inventor improved Navy's biscuits', *HM*, February 1985

Chapter 6: Feeding the Guns

Allen, L., *The History of Portsmouth* (1817)

Gates, W. (1900)

Hoad, M., 'Portsmouth as others have seen it 1540-1790', *PP*, No. 15 (1972)

Ministry of Defence, *A Guide to RNAD Gosport* (c.1990)

Quennell, M. and C., *A History of Everyday Things in England* (1924)

Sadden, J., *Keep the Home Fires Burning* (1990)

Saunders, W.H., *Annals of Portsmouth* (1880)

Sewmark, H. W., *The R.N. Armament Depots of Priddy's Hard, Elson, Frater & Bedenham* (1977)

White, W., *Hampshire Gazetteer and Directory* (1878)

Chapter 7: Naval Recruitment and Education

Allen, L., *The History of Portsmouth* (1817)

Cooper, C.G., *HMS Fisgard at Gosport*, GOS, No. 12, December 1976

Gates, W. (1900)

Horn, R.S., *HM Naval Base, Portsmouth – a description of some of the historic buildings in the Conservation Area* (1975)

Hutchinson, J.R., *The press gang afloat and ashore* (1913)

Ireland, J., 'Stubbington House School – a cradle of the Navy', *HM*, February 1990

Lambert, R., 'Academy's chequered past', *First Base*, July 1995

'The Royal Naval College, Portsmouth', *NAI*, 2 July 1898

'Naval education a hundred years ago', *NR*, Vol. 42 (1954)

Owen, H., 'Eastman's Royal Naval Academy, Southsea, in the 1870s', *MM*, Vol. 77, No. 4, November 1991

Pearce, J., 'The hard way at Hardway', *HM*, February 1977

Pococke, R., in Hoad, M., 'Portsmouth as others have seen it 1540-1790', *PP*, No.15 (1972)

Prestidge, C., *A History of Stubbington*, 2nd ed. (1996)

Rodger, N.A.M., *The Wooden World: An Anatomy of the Georgian Navy* (1986)

Schofield, B., *Navigation and Direction – The Story of HMS Dryad* (1977)

Chapter 8: Naval Gunnery Training

'Excellent by name ...', *First Base*, Issue 2, November 1995

Warlow, B., *Shore Establishments of the Royal Navy* (1992)

Young, R. Travers, *The House that Jack Built* (1955)

Chapter 9: Underwater Warfare: Mines, Torpedoes and Submarines

Burton, L., *Gosport Goes to War* (1981)

Compton-Hall, R., *Fort Blockhouse*, GOS, No.12 (1976)

HMS *Dolphin, Submarine open-day* (leaflet) (*c*.1972)

Donnithorne, C., *Fort Blockhouse* (leaflet) (*c*.2000)

Harfield, A., 'Dress of the Militia Officers of the Submarine Miners', *Military Historical Society*, Vol XXXV, No. 137

Harfield, A., 'Monckton's Miners', *HM*, May 1986

'HMS Vernon', *NR*, Vol. 42 (1954)

Preston, A. and Batchelor, J., *The First Submarines* (undated)

Ripley, B., 'Horsea Island and the Royal Navy', *PP*, No. 36 (1982)

Wadlow, E., 'Wartime memories of Leigh Park House', *HM*, February 1987

Warner W.E., *A Short History of Fort Blockhouse* (1947)

Webb, E.D., *HMS Vernon 1930-1955* (1956)

Chapter 10: Air Defence

Newberry, D., *Naval Aviation at Lee on Solent* (undated, *c*.1996)

PN Centenary Supplement (April 1977)

'Pioneer pilot records Gosport's contribution to military aviation', *PN*, 30 March 1976

Parfoot, J.D., *A Touch of History – The Story of Gosport Airfield* (1998)

Stanley, A., 'Flying into fame', *Yesterday*, December 1990

Webster, E., 'Where the Navy found its wings – 50 years ago', *HM*, November 1965

Chapter 11: Naval Communication, Navigation and Radar

'HM Navigation School 1903-68', *NR*, Vol. LVI, No. 3, July 1968

Ripley, B., 'Horsea Island and the Royal Navy', *PP*, No. 36 (1982)

Dwyer, D.J., *A history of the Royal Naval Barracks, Portsmouth* (1961)

ARE, *Admiralty Research Establishment, Portsdown* (1985)

Vidler, N., *The story of ASWE* (1969)

Chapter 12: Naval Barracks and Other Establishments

Dannreuther, H. E., *R.N. Barracks, Portsmouth and its History* (1932)

Lambert, J. and Ross, A., *Allied Coastal Forces of World War II, Vol. II, Vosper MTBs and US Elcos* (1993)

Brown, D.K., 'R.E. Froude and the shape of warships', *Journal of Nautical Science*, Vol. 13, No. 3

Burton, L., *Haslar's Historic Ship Tank*, GOS, No. 3, 1972

Burton, L., 'The Admiralty Research Establishment, Haslar' in Burton, L. (ed.), *Attentive to our duty* (1986)

Cook, T. and Lelion, E., 'Hydrodynamic test facilities at ARE (Haslar) Part 1 – Ship Tanks', *Journal of Nautical Science*, Vol. 13, No. 1

Defence Evaluation & Research Agency, *Annual Report 1998/99* (1999)

Focus on Industrial Archaeology, The Froude Testing Tank at Haslar, No. 41, January 1994

Nepean, A., 'Naval R & D Establishments – Are there too many?', *Navy International*, Vol. 83, August 1978

Otter, R.A. (ed.), *Civil Engineering Heritage – Southern England* (1990)

Benson, M.G.W., *HMS Hornet*, GOS, No. 5

'Gosport's gallant little boats', *PN*, 14 February 1975

Dicker, S., *Vernon* (1972)

HMS *Sultan, Hon Freedom of Borough of Gosport* (1975)

Chapter 13: Off Duty

Dwyer, D.J., *A History of the Royal Navy Barracks, Portsmouth* (1961)

Gulliver, Doris, *Dame Agnes Weston* (1971)

Taylor, M.W., 'Sarah Robinson – the Soldier's Friend'. *HM*, January 1965

Weston, A., *My Life with the Bluejackets* (1909)

Chapter 14: Naval and Military Hospitals

Burton, L., *Gosport Goes to War* (1981)

Gange, M., *The Hospitals of Portsmouth Past and Present* (1988)

Lloyd, C., 'The health of seamen', *NRS*, Vol. CVII, 1965

Ministry of Defence, *Institute of Naval Medicine* (1988)

'Haslar Hospital', *NAI*, 19 February 1897

PRC (1835-1927) (1928-30) (1946-55)

Purvis, G., 'The History of St James' Hospital' (1977, unpublished)

Revell, A.L., *Haslar – the Royal Hospital* (c.1978)

Sadden, J., *Keep the Home Fires Burning – the story of Portsmouth and Gosport in World War 1* (1990)

Tait, W., *A History of Haslar* (1906)

White, W., *History of Hampshire – Gazetteer and Directory* (1878)

Chapter 15: Fleet Reviews and Military Displays

PRC (1835-1927) (1928-30)

Kemp, P.K., *Some Naval Reviews of the Past* (1953)

Patterson, A. Temple, 'Palmerston's Folly – The Portsdown and Spithead Forts', *PP*, No. 3 (1970)

INDEX

Numbers in *italic* refer to illustrations.

View of men leaving Portsmouth Harbour for the Baltic Fleet which was anchored at Spithead, 1855.